LMS Steam Revi

ABOVE: LMS 'Crab' 2-6-0 No. 13065, 3F 'Jinty' 0-6-0T No. 16410 and L&Y 0-6-0 No. 12322 at Buckley Wells shed on the East Lancashire Railway in November 2014. ROBERT FALCONER

THE LONDON Midland and Scottish Railway was the largest of the Big Four companies formed by the grouping of Britain's independent railway companies in 1923. It could trace its ancestry back to Stephenson's *Rocket*'s success at Rainhill, leading to the construction of the world's first inter-city railway from Liverpool to Manchester in 1830.

The LMS comprised mainly of the Midland Railway, the London & North Western Railway, which had already absorbed the Lancashire & Yorkshire Railway, and the Caledonian, Glasgow & South Western and Highland railways in Scotland. Smaller companies were the Furness, North Staffordshire, London Tilbury & Southend, and North London railways; it also had an interest in the Somerset & Dorset Joint, as well as the Midland & Great Northern Joint railways.

Its arch-rival the London & North Eastern Railway, had the two most famous steam engines in the world in the 1930s; *Flying Scotsman* and speed record holder *Mallard*, and is also now represented in preservation by the new Pacific *Tornado*. The LMS did not have engines which quite caught the imagination of the public in the same way, though it was not for lack of trying.

Fowler's Royal Scot built in 1927 for the 'Royal Scot' service from Euston to Glasgow was impressive. The LMS had a close affinity with royalty and the military and the Patriot and Silver Jubilee locomotive names continued this theme. The Stanier Pacific Coronation, built in 1937 for the 'Coronation Scot' service to Glasgow was eye-catching in its blue streamlined guise, and it was fast and powerful. In the end though it could not match *Mallard* for speed.

The early days of the LMS were typified by inter-company rivalry, with the philosophies of the Midland and the LNWR proving incompatible for many years, and a huge collection of often archaic, non-standard and underpowered steam engines took a long time to give way to more modern standard types.

Nevertheless, impressive maroon engines doing battle with the wild terrain and fearsome gradients of Shap and Ais Gill, Beattock, Drumochter and Slochd and the steepest of them all the Lickey incline, are what the LMS is remembered for. Much of this atmosphere was carried through into BR steam days and remarkably is recaptured regularly by the steam preservation movement today.

Stations such as Euston, St Pancras, Birmingham New Street, Crewe, Carlisle Citadel, Glasgow Central, Holyhead and Thurso, served by trains such as the 'Royal Scot' and 'Caledonian', 'Thames-Clyde Express' and 'Waverley', 'Irish Mail', 'Pines Express' and 'Orcadian' give the LMS a well-deserved place in railway history.

We are lucky that such a variety of LMS steam power has survived to see use in the preservation era. The LMS was traditionally not good at preserving its heritage and even scrapped engines at Derby that had been considered for preservation. BR tended to carry on this tradition, not keeping any LMS express engines, scrapping a Highland 4-4-0 in 1967 and even demolishing both Euston and Birmingham New Street stations.

Nevertheless 116 steam engines of LMS or its constituent's designs are still in existence today, no fewer than 79 of which have been steamed in preservation. This is the story of all those engines.

AUTHOR: Brian Sharpe

DESIGN: Panda Media/Sarah Palmer

PRODUCTION EDITOR: Sarah Palmer

COVER DESIGN: Michael Baumber

REPROGRAPHICS: Jonathan Schofield

PUBLISHER: Tim Hartley

COMMERICIAL DIRECTOR: Nigel Hole

PUBLISHING DIRECTOR: Dan Savage

PUBLISHED BY: Mortons Media Group Ltd, Media Centre, Morton Way, Horncastle, Lincolnshire, LN9 6JR

Tel: 01507 529529

PRINTED BY: William Gibbons And Sons, Wolverhampton

CREDITS: All photographs are the author's unless otherwise stated.

ISBN: 978 1 909128 71 2

MEDIA GROUP LTD

Contents

MAIN PHOTO: LMS Princess Royal Pacific No. 46203 *Princess Margaret Rose* and Princess Coronation No. 46233 *Duchess of Sutherland* at Swanwick Junction on the Midland Railway-Butterley in November 2014. JOHN TITLOW
FAR LEFT: LMS Streamlined Princess Coronation Pacific No. 6229 *Duchess of Hamilton* and Princess Royal No. 6201 *Princess Elizabeth* at the National Railway Museum's Railfest at York in 2012.
COVER PIC: LMS 4-6-0 No. 46100 *Royal Scot* passes through Oldbury cutting near Bridgnorth, during the Severn Valley Railway's autumn gala on September 18, 2015. PHIL JONES

CHAPTER I

LMS heritage railways

ABOVE: LMS Ivatt 2MT 2-6-2T No. 41241 and SR USA 0-6-0T No. 72 at Oxenhope with the Keighley & Worth Valley Railway reopening train on June 29, 1968. GAVIN MORRISON

Keighley & Worth Valley Railway

THE FIVE-mile Worth Valley branch south from Keighley in West Yorkshire was opened on April 15, 1867 by local businessmen and mill owners. It climbs steeply at 1-in-58 up the valley to Oakworth, then to Haworth, famous as the home of the Brontë sisters, and on to the terminus at Oxenhope.

At Keighley, it connected with the Midland Railway main line from Leeds to Skipton and Carlisle. Eventually the MR bought out the KWVR and the line became part of the LMS but falling traffic led to its early closure by BR, first to passengers in December 1961 and then to goods in June 1962.

However, following the success of pioneer preservationists in North Wales and the reopening of the five-mile Bluebell Railway in Sussex local people and enthusiasts formed a preservation society to save the Worth Valley branch on a similar basis. A company

was created to buy the line itself, and lease the access to Keighley station where it could continue to connect with the main line.

When the line closed, it was in a poor state, but from 1965 locomotives and rolling stock started to be assembled in Haworth yard, which was to become the headquarters, and occasional steam days were held. After six years of hard work by volunteers, the line was reopened on June 29, 1968. The KWVR became Britain's second standard gauge preserved steam railway to operate a regular passenger service on former main line track, just eight years after the Bluebell line. The reopening train was headed by former Skipton-based LMS Ivatt 2-6-2T No. 41241 in maroon livery and SR USA 0-6-0T No. 72 in orange livery and was formed of vintage stock.

The new KWVR paid BR for the line in instalments over 25 years, the purchase being completed in 1992. Since reopening, the line

has been unique among major heritage lines in being operated entirely by volunteers. It is an ideal self-contained branch line, in a popular tourist area but close to a very densely populated conurbation. It can never be extended but the ride is long enough and surprisingly varied.

The locomotive stock has steadily expanded and motive power is often of appropriate LMS heritage, if somewhat larger than would have been seen in steam days with some of Britain's largest express engines having occasionally found their way up the branch.

The line still has a physical connection with Network Rail and railtours occasionally start from or run to Oxenhope.

The KWVR has remained one of the country's premier heritage railways and the journey in a typical 1950s train of maroon coaches hauled by a black steam engine is a reminder of our industrial heritage.

ABOVE: Lancashire & Yorkshire Railway A class 0-6-0 No. 52322 departs from Bolton Abbey on the Embsay & Bolton Abbey Steam Railway.

Embsay & Bolton Abbey Steam Railway

THE 11-mile Ilkley to Skipton line was opened on October 1, 1888 by the MR, but was closed in March 1965 east of Embsay Junction, a branch remaining to the north of Embsay serving the limestone quarry near Grassington. The Embsay & Grassington Railway Preservation Society was formed in October 1968 to preserve the Grassington branch.

The line did not close so the society changed its name to the Yorkshire Dales Railway and set its sights on part of the MR Skipton to Ilkley line instead, although there was only 880 yards of track left. It took occupation of what was left of Embsay station in 1970. Track was laid, buildings restored and locomotives and stock assembled so that steam trains could start to operate even if only on a limited basis.

July 1987 saw trains running from Embsay as far as Holywell, and to Stoneacre in 1991, by which time the line had rebranded itself as the Embsay Steam Railway. By 1997, the railway had extended as far as Bolton Abbey giving a four-mile run, and a superb replica of the original station was constructed.

Although more of a main line than a branch line, unlike the KWVR, the EBAR's motive power has tended to be of industrial origin, although main line power does make regular appearances, particularly for gala weekends. The line also has potential to extend further towards Ilkley and there are even proposals for running into Skipton itself.

Midland Railway-Butterley

AMONG THE many preservation schemes that blossomed around the time of the end of BR steam, this one was different. Rather than setting out to save a particular stretch of line, the proposal was to commemorate the role of the Midland Railway in the industrial history of Derby.

This led to a decision in 1969 by Derby Corporation to create a museum dedicated to the history and development of the Midland Railway, its predecessors and successors. The project was supported by the Midland Railway Project Group; a voluntary organisation set up to collect and restore exhibits and operating equipment. Derby Corporation arranged to purchase two LMS 3F 'Jinty' 0-6-0Ts from Woodham's scrapyard at Barry and another was purchased from the National Coal Board.

The site eventually chosen was a 3½-mile section of the Pye Bridge-Ambergate line that had closed in 1968. Unfortunately the realignment of the A610 had taken up most of the trackbed between Hammersmith and Ambergate.

Work started on the site in 1973 only for both the county council and Derby Corporation to withdraw through lack of funds. However, volunteers decided to continue and the Midland Railway Trust was formed on December 9, 1976. Whitwell station building was rebuilt on the demolished Butterley station site and in 1975 the first steam open day was held.

The first public passenger train ran over a mile of track on August 22, 1981 and services were gradually extended from Butterley, west to Hammersmith and east to near Pye Bridge, where a connection with the Erewash Valley main line has been maintained. The railway now has an unrivalled collection of stations, signalboxes and signalling equipment of MR origin plus a large museum building and workshops plus much more besides.

Swanwick Junction also became home to the Princess Royal Class Locomotive Trust, owner of two LMS Pacifics and two BR Standard 2-6-4Ts, all of which have seen regular main line use. The line is short but recaptures much of the atmosphere of one of Britain's most distinctive pre-Grouping railway companies.

BELOW: 3F 0-6-0T No. 47357 departs from Hammersmith at the Midland Railway Centre on May 22, 2002.

Peak Rail

ONE OF the saddest losses as a result of the Beeching cuts of the 1960s was the spectacularly scenic section of the Midland Railway main line from Derby to Manchester, which closed completely in June 1968 between Matlock and Millers Dale Junction, with the sections from there to Buxton, and north through Peak Forest to Chinley only being retained for freight.

At the time, preservation societies were thinking in terms of five-mile branch lines as heritage steam railways, and taking over a 15-mile stretch of double-track main line with substantial tunnels and viaducts, running into main line stations at each end was not considered a practical proposition.

By 1975 attitudes had changed slightly and aims were more ambitious. A society was formed to reopen the Matlock to Buxton line, the trackbed of which remained available. The society initially established a site at Buxton with a 300yd operating line and reinstated a missing bridge with a view to extending its track alongside the freight-only line through Ashwood Dale towards Millers Dale, but this wasn't successful.

In the 1980s Peak Rail relocated its headquarters to Darley Dale near Matlock and by 1991 had reopened the line from there to Matlock Riverside. In 1997, it was extended northwards to within half a mile of the original Rowsley station and a new station was constructed next to the site of the former Rowsley shed.

A new track layout was installed between Matlock Riverside and Network Rail's Matlock station to maintain the connection to the national network and this was finally reopened on July 2, 2011.

The preserved line now runs for 3½ miles but is operated largely by industrial or diesel power. However, main line locomotives occasionally visit, sometimes on railtours from the national network.

In 2004, Derbyshire County Council published a study, which concluded that reopening the former line for a local service was technically feasible and that the trackbed should remain clear of development, but it was not an economic possibility in the near future.

The railway still intends to extend its services northward to Bakewell if possible. Beyond Bakewell the trackbed is used by the hugely popular Monsal Trail footpath and cycleway but a restored line could still operate a single track alongside it.

Nevertheless, huge sums of money are required, as a bridge over the A6 needs to be built at Rowsley. If it had developed as intended, Peak Rail could have become the best-preserved railway in Britain, but so far it has not happened.

ABOVE: Newly restored maroon-liveried LMS 8F 2-8-0 No. 8624 on the turntable at Rowsley on Peak Rail. MIKE HOWKINS

Battlefield Line

THE ASHBY & Nuneaton Joint Railway was the only major line built jointly by the MR and LNWR, opening in 1873, and not actually passing through Ashby-de-la-Zouch. Primarily built for coal traffic, passenger services ceased in 1931 and the Coalville-Shackerstone line closed completely in 1964, although the Ashby-Nuneaton line lasted until early 1970.

Shackerstone station became the headquarters of what was later known as the Market Bosworth Light Railway and is now known as the Battlefield Line, with trains running south via Market Bosworth, to Shenton, the site of the famous Battle of Bosworth in 1485.

Trains started running in the 1970s but the line led a relatively low-key existence until recent years when main line motive power has become a much more regular feature, with some interesting visitors for gala events.

RIGHT: LNWR Coal Tank 0-6-2T No. 1054 departs from Market Bosworth on the Battlefield Line on March 21, 1997. MALCOLM RANIERI

Avon Valley Railway

THE MIDLAND Railway extended from Carlisle to London but also to Bristol. A branch from Mangotsfield near Bristol giving the company a route into Bath opened on August 4, 1869, running parallel to the GWR main line.

The line closed to passengers under the Beeching cuts on March 7, 1966, although coal traffic to Bath gasworks continued until July 1971, after which the track was lifted. In a slightly unusual move a group of local people with the then local MP Robert Adley set up the Bristol Suburban Railway Society to reopen the route; a Midland line in the middle of GWR territory.

The society based itself at Bitton station and so the Bristol Suburban Railway Society became the Bitton Railway Co in 1979 and now markets itself as the Avon Valley Railway. Three miles of track have so far been reinstated and motive power is predominantly industrial with occasional main line visitors.

LEFT: The restoration of LMS 'Black Five' 4-6-0 No. 45379 from Barry scrapyard condition commenced at Bitton and the engine was able to return for a working visit from the Mid Hants Railway on October 15, 2011. CLIFF THOMAS

Chasewater Light Railway

THE HISTORY of this little steam railway can be traced back to the early days of standard gauge preservation. The Railway Preservation Society was the idea of Noel Draycott in 1959, who wanted a co-ordinated plan for private railway preservation, not lots of independent groups. The West Midlands Group of the RPS acquired a site at Hednesford in Staffordshire, bought a couple of six-wheeled coaches from the NCB and briefly had custody of LNWR Webb Coal Tank 0-6-2T No. 1054.

Other possible lines were considered but the then Aldridge-Brownhills Urban District Council was developing a pleasure park at Chasewater and part of the adjacent trackbed of a former MR line was available for lease, this being signed in December 1964.

Track was laid and the first steam open day was held on June 29, 1968, after which Hednesford closed and industrial locomotives and stock were concentrated at Chasewater. The frequency of services increased but

passenger numbers dwindled and the line closed in October 1982, not restarting until three years later, since when the line has seen a remarkable resurgence.

Stations and signalboxes have been built and the running line extended. It is not recognisable as the original MR route and architecture is predominantly LNWR. Motive power is normally industrial or diesel but it is another diverse part of the one-time LMS still seeing regular steam working.

Nene Valley Railway

THE NVR's main running line from Peterborough to Yarwell Mill was built by the London & Birmingham Railway and later formed part of the LNWR.

The LBR line was opened from Blisworth on the West Coast Main Line to Peterborough in 1845, making an end-on connection with the Eastern Counties Railway and briefly forming the city's rail link with the capital, until the GNR line from King's Cross was opened.

The line split at Yarwell Junction, with routes to Northampton and to Rugby, the latter forming the main rail link from Birmingham to East Anglia. Northampton trains ceased in 1964 and Rugby trains two years later with through services diverted via Leicester, but freight traffic continued to Oundle until 1972. The Peterborough Development Corporation acquired the double-track line that ran through the proposed Nene Park, part of the plan for the doubling of the size of the city.

A local vicar, Rev Richard Paten, had bought a BR Standard 5MT 4-6-0, No. 73050, from BR in 1968 and from this grew the Nene Valley Railway, which reopened more than the five miles from Orton Mere to Wansford in May 1977, initially using predominantly

ABOVE: LMS 'Black Five' 4-6-0 No. 5231 heads west from Peterborough on the Nene Valley Railway in May 1992.

continental locomotives and stock. The line was extended east from Orton Mere into Peterborough in 1986 and west from Wansford to Yarwell to give a length of 7½ miles. It has seen a steady flow of visiting locomotives with LMS power ranging from 4F 0-6-0 No. 44422 to Pacific No. 46229 *Duchess of Hamilton*.

There was initially no direct connection between the LBR and GNR but a 1¼-mile loop line was built later by the GNR.

This branch from Longueville Junction, which now forms the line's connection with Network Rail, is used for stock movements and occasional railtours.

Northampton & Lamport Railway

THE NORTHAMPTON to Market Harborough line was opened by the LNWR in 1859 and although closed to passenger traffic on January 4, 1960, it was reopened for through traffic briefly in 1969 and again in 1972-73, being a useful diversionary route.

In June 1981 the Welland Valley Railway Revival Group was set up with the aim of reopening as much of the line as possible, as it was then about to finally close to freight traffic. It became the Northampton Steam Railway and then the Northampton & Lamport Railway, based at Pitsford & Brampton station, five miles north of Northampton.

The trackbed was purchased from BR by Northampton County Council and converted to a cycleway, but the NLR carried its first passengers on a short section of track on November 19, 1995. The running line has slowly been extended and further extension is planned, but motive power has been predominantly industrial or diesel, although LMS 3F 'Jinty' 0-6-0T No. 47298 paid a short visit in 1996.

ABOVE: LMS 'Jinty' 0-6-0T No. 47298 heads south on the Northampton & Lamport Railway in April 1996. JOHN PEPPER / NLR

Lakeside & Haverthwaite Railway

THE FURNESS Railway main line ran from Carnforth round the Cumbrian Coast to Barrow-in-Furness and Whitehaven. Among its branches was one from Plumpton Junction to a terminus at the south end of Lake Windermere where passengers could board the steamers, which had sailed around the lake after 1850. This eight-mile branch opened on June 1, 1869, and its main revenue was always from freight traffic.

The FR bought the steamers and enjoyed some profitable years from the tourist traffic but the line was closed to passengers by BR on September 5, 1965 though freight continued to Haverthwaite and Backbarrow until April 2, 1967.

Austin Maher, a Lancashire businessman and his brother Charles, a farmer from near Kendal were introduced to Dr Peter Beet and John Parkin, who were interested in reopening the Lakeside branch as a steam railway. The Lakeside Railway Estates Company was formed with Dr Beet as chairman and John Parkin as a director, later joined by Austin and others.

Unfortunately the Lake District planning board wanted to convert the trackbed of the Haverthwaite to Lakeside section into a footpath, and BR was obliged to consider this proposal in preference to that of the Lakeside Railway Company. Considerable lobbying at the highest level was needed before the planning board withdrew its opposition to the railway in 1969.

By then though, the trunk road authorities had made it known that they wished to use large sections of the trackbed for improvements to the A590 trunk road. They were prepared to build a couple of bridges to avoid obliterating the line completely but only if the railway company paid for them. The company clearly could not afford this and abandoned the scheme.

ABOVE: Caledonian blue-liveried LMS Fairburn 2-6-4T No. 2085 departs from Haverthwaite on May 9, 1976.

However, two of the company's directors, Jim Morris and Austin Maher together with David Piercy, formed the Lakeside and Haverthwaite Railway Company Ltd to try to save the northern 3½-mile section from Haverthwaite to Lakeside, supported by the Lakeside Railway Society.

The bridges were not built, of course; the rest of the branch was lost but at least Haverthwite station and its site remained intact.

BR agreed a sale of this section in 1970. Locomotives had been purchased and were stored at Steamtown Carnforth, and these were delivered by rail late that year before the line was finally severed.

Austin, who had also been responsible for funding all the administration expenses of the previous years, then purchased the Lakeside and Haverthwaite Railway, and the line reopened on May 2, 1973, the reopening train being headed by two LMS Fairburn 4MT 2-6-4Ts Nos. 2073 and 2085.

These unique engines have formed the backbone of the main line locomotive fleet ever since although industrial power has inevitably predominated, being more economical for short journeys.

ABOVE: MR Compound 4-4-0 No. 1000 under the coaling tower at Steamtown Carnforth on May 5, 1980.

Steamtown Carnforth

A NEW steam locomotive shed was constructed alongside the WCML at Carnforth as late as 1944 replacing the previous LNWR building, which was undersized to deal with a boom in traffic in the area during the war. The adjacent station was a junction where the Furness main line met the LNWR main line over Shap, and became famous as the setting for the film Brief Encounter.

As the shed was so much more modern than others in the area, despite being oversized after the end of the war, BR increasingly concentrated more of its steam servicing at Carnforth (10A) until it became one of the last three steam sheds in Britain, finally closing on August 4, 1968.

By then Dr Peter Beet had formed the Lakeside Railway Estates Company, initially to preserve the Lakeside branch from Plumpton Junction. As negotiations proved protracted, locomotives were being stored in the meantime at Carnforth; Dr Beet's LMS Ivatt 2-6-0 No. 6441 in ornate LMS maroon livery rubbing shoulders with the last of BR's 'Black Five' 4-6-0s and others after 1967. A last-minute flurry of activity at the very end of steam saw several 'Black Fives' purchased for preservation at the end and, with the site leased from BR, steam open days were held, with the venue acquiring the name Steamtown.

However, when it proved impossible to save the whole of the Lakeside branch, Dr Beet's company pulled out. The new company, which preserved only part of the branch,

moved its four engines to the line in 1970, but the rest stayed at Carnforth and Steamtown and therefore continued on a more permanent basis than perhaps originally envisaged, under Dr Beet's leadership. It was developed as a major visitor attraction, and went on to acquire express Pacifics from France and Germany.

1972 saw the lifting of BR's ban on the operation of privately owned steam engines on the main line, and some of Carnforth's 'Black Fives' returned to main line action. In 1974 Sir William McAlpine bought an interest in the company, as he needed a base for LNER A3 Pacific No. 4472 Flying Scotsman, which he had saved after its troubles in America. The A3 was based at Steamtown for many years with McAlpine securing a controlling interest in the company, after which he purchased the site.

Steamtown became the premier main line steam operating base in Britain, partly as a result of BR's reluctance to encourage too much steam activity further south. Things changed though; Dr Beet moved his engines away in 1990, and McAlpine's interest declined after No. 4472's move south in 1986 where there was now more potential business.

Although main line steam operations were handled by BR, after Privatisation freight company English Welsh & Scottish Railways took over in the 1990s, however, the West Coast Railway company set up by businessman, David Smith, and based at Carnforth mounted a successful challenge to what appeared to be a monopoly situation. It

became a Train Operating Company in its own right and has built up its business to become the dominant main line steam operator in Britain, ensuring that big LMS steam power can be enjoyed, on the Settle & Carlisle especially, several times a week in the summer months. Active engines now on West Coast's books have been supplemented by Jubilee No. 45699 Galatea and Royal Scot No. 46115 Scots Guardsman.

The poor condition of Carnforth's shed building though, led to its closure as a public attraction, and it is now purely a private site.

ABOVE: LMS Royal Scot 4-6-0 No. 46115 Scots Guardsman and Jubilee 4-6-0 No. 5690 Leander during a West Coast Railways' open day at Carnforth in July 2008.

BELOW: LMS 4F 0-6-0 No. 44422 passes Burrs on the East Lancashire Railway with an early-morning goods train in January 2006.

East Lancashire Railway

ALTHOUGH THE ELR only opened for regular passenger services in 1987 and is considered a late starter in preservation terms, it can be considered the premier LMS heritage line with its origins going back further than is generally realised.

The railway geography of North Lancashire is complicated; Bury was at the crossroads of the L&Y's north-south Manchester to Accrington line and its east-west original East Lancashire line from Bolton to Rochdale.

The beginnings of the 'new' ELR can be traced back to the arrival of LMS 'Black Five' 4-6-0 No. 44806 at Accrington in 1970. The plan then was for a heritage line from Accrington to Helmshore but this came to nothing and the 4-6-0 quickly moved to Haverthwaite. In 1982, BR finally stopped running coal trains north of Bury to Rawtenstall; the end of a branch off the Accrington line that originally served Bacup. The ELR commenced services from Bolton Street station at Bury, then as far as Ramsbottom on July 25, 1987, extending to Rawtenstall in 1991.

Bolton Street station had been abandoned by BR as the Manchester Metrolink tram system reached Bury over the original L&Y railway route but had been diverted to terminate in a new transport interchange at Bury. There had always been an intention to extend the line by turning through 90° to the east south of Bolton Street to gain the route to Castleton where connection could be made with Network Rail's Calder Valley main line.

The track was upgraded for passenger services to run as far as Heywood where a station was built, giving a 12-mile 'L-shaped' run from September 2003. However, once on the original ELR route, the extension had to cross over the new Metrolink tram route at the site of Knowsley Street station. This necessitated the construction of a new overbridge, between two major road bridges

leading to gradients of 1-in-36 and 1-in-41 either side of the new bridge.

The railway set up its workshops in the large complex that once included Bury steam shed at Buckley Wells, but engineer and locomotive owner Ian Riley's company took over a major part of the largest building from where it carries out major contract overhauls of main line steam locomotives. It is also a base for the company's main line certified steam locomotives, which see intensive use on main line steam railtour operations.

Churnet Valley Railway

THE NORTH Staffordshire Railway's secondary main line from Uttoxeter to Macclesfield via Leek formed part of the shortest route from London and Derby to Manchester when it opened in 1849. Under the Beeching cuts, when it closed to passengers; an interesting network of lines to the east of Stoke-on-Trent was retained to serve stone quarries on the edge of the Staffordshire moorlands.

A preservation society established a base at Cheddleton in the 1970s with a view to reopening part of the NSR route in the event of the stone traffic ceasing; this eventually happened, but not until August 1988.

Four years later the company applied to for a Light Railway Order to enable it to operate the CVR line, and in 1995 agreement was reached with BR for the purchase of part of the line, subject to raising sufficient capital. A major share issue was launched, which was well supported, and raised more than £120,000.

In total the Churnet Valley Railway Company purchased seven miles of trackbed from Leekbrook through Cheddleton to Oakamoor and ran its first passenger train on August 24, 1996 over the one-mile section from Cheddleton to Leekbrook. Services were extended south to Consall Forge on July 11, 1998.

The line was further extended south to Kingsley & Froghall where a new station was built but regular services have never run beyond here to Oakamoor. Meanwhile though a new separate company, Moorland and City Railways was set up with the aim of

reopening the rest of the disused track from Leekbrook Junction, east to Cauldon Lowe and west into Stoke-on-Trent, and possibly to relay track north into Leek. Key to the success of this ambitious plan was to re-establish the stone traffic from Cauldon Lowe and the company was successful in bringing the track up to standard for a high-profile launch of a steam service from the CVR beyond Leekbrook Junction and up the steep climb towards Cauldon Lowe in November 2010.

However, in 2014, the track was lifted beyond Ipstones summit because of its poor condition, while only slow progress has been made with upgrading the track towards Stoke-on-Trent.

ABOVE: Newly restored LNWR 'Super D' 0-8-0 No. 49395 passes Thomas Bolton's wire works as it departs from Kingsley & Froghall on the Churnet Valley Railway in June 2004.

Ribble Steam Railway

THE RIBBLE Steam Railway grew from the ashes of the Steamport Railway Museum at Southport, which closed in 1999, leaving a large collection of locomotives looking for a new home. Preston Docks was chosen as the new location as it had once had a large railway network.

The new site was redeveloped; the first building to open being the workshop in 2001, with a museum completed in 2004. With one of the largest collections of locomotives in Britain, the railway opened to the public on September 17, 2005, running alongside the western part of the LNWR's docks branch starting from Preston station.

Bitumen trains still use the branch during the week with the RSR running its trains at weekends, and even main line railtours have been operated to Preston Riverside. Although relatively short it is one of Britain's most unusual heritage lines and does see main line motive power on occasions.

RIGHT: L&Y 0-6-0 No. 12322 crosses the unique swing bridge in Preston docks on the Ribble Steam Railway. FRED KERR

Strathspey Railway

BUILDING A RAILWAY from Perth to Inverness through the inhospitable terrain of the Scottish Highlands in the early years of the railway boom was considered too ambitious by many, but in 1863 a line was opened running via Aviemore, Grantown and Forres, which became the main line of the Highland Railway in 1865.

In 1898 though, the Highland did what had earlier appeared impossible and opened a more direct line from Aviemore to Inverness via Carrbridge. The original line from Aviemore through Grantown-on-Spey was relegated to a secondary route, and this line eventually fell victim to the Beeching axe with passenger services being withdrawn in 1965 and complete closure coming three years later.

The Strathspey Railway Company was established in 1971 with the aim of reopening part of the original line and in the following year agreed to purchase the trackbed from Aviemore to Grantown from BR. Reinstating even part of the route was nearly as ambitious as building the original railway but after years of hard work, trains ran again from a new station near Aviemore as far as Boat of Garten in 1978. In 1998, trains started running into

Platform 3 of the main line station and in 2002, the line was extended from Boat of Garten to Broomhill.

It is still intended to extend to Grantown, where the station has disappeared, and good progress is being made with replacing the missing bridge over the Dulnain River. In a popular tourist area, the Strathspey Railway has grown to become the main Scottish venue for the operation of LMS steam power.

ABOVE: CR 0-6-0 No. 828 departs from Boat of Garten on the Strathspey Railway in October 2010.

Caledonian Railway

THE CALEDONIAN RAILWAY runs on four miles of former CR track between Brechin and Bridge of Dun in Angus, Scotland.

This line was originally built in 1848 and became part of the original Caledonian Railway in 1865, Bridge of Dun being a junction on its main line from Glasgow to Aberdeen.

The line closed to passengers in 1952 but freight traffic was still running up the branch in 1979 the same year as a preservation society was set up and the first steam engine arrived at Brechin. Closure by BR came in 1981 but it took 13 years of hard work before the society ran its first passenger trains along the branch in 1992.

Brechin station survived as a classic CR branch terminus but motive power has been predominantly industrial or diesel with only the very occasional main line visitor.

LEFT: CR 0-4-4T No. 419 on a short visit to the Caledonian Railway at Brechin on August 4, 2002. IAN LOTHIAN

Steamport Southport

THE SOUTHPORT Railway Museum (Steamport) was based in the Lancashire and Yorkshire Railway engine shed at Southport (27C). The project was first started in 1973, with the preservation centre opening on the Derby Road in the town.

However, the shed became too costly for the museum to maintain, and although negotiations continued, an offer for the site from a property developer tipped the balance and a decision was made to relocate the collection with the museum closing in 1999.

Liverpool Road Station

LIVERPOOL ROAD was the Manchester terminus of the world's first inter-city passenger railway and is now the world's oldest-surviving railway terminus, built in 1830 but closed to passenger services on May 4, 1844 and converted to a goods yard.

When BR closed this and its warehouses in 1975, parts were purchased by Granada Television, some being used for the set of TV soap Coronation Street, but Greater Manchester Council purchased the earliest part from BR in 1978 and a museum was opened on September 15, 1983.

The station, which is Grade I listed, is part of the Museum of Science and Industry in Manchester (MOSI), originally called the North Western Museum of Science and Industry. It has operated short steam train rides, some hauled by *Planet*, a replica of Robert Stephenson's Planet class 2-2-0, built by the Friends of the Museum of Science and Industry in 1992.

Liverpool Road station has, up to now, retained main line rail access. However, this will no longer be possible as Network Rail is building a new length of main line across it, which has severely curtailed railway operations.

Crewe Heritage Centre

THE CENTRE WAS opened on June 24, 1987 in a part of Crewe locomotive works no longer required by BR, just north of Crewe station.

It rebranded to its original name of Crewe Heritage Centre in early 2008 and has a number of exhibits, including the prototype Advanced Passenger Train, miniature railways, and three signalboxes. It is open to the public on summer weekends and often plays host to main line steam locomotives.

Alongside the heritage centre, another part of Crewe works was established as the engineering arm of Waterman Railways, which was established by Pete Waterman. This part of the business developed as the London & North Western Railway Company, and was responsible for major overhauls of preserved locomotives both for Waterman Railways and outside contracts, particularly heavy boiler overhauls.

2014 though saw the business sold to Jeremy Hosking's Royal Scot Locomotive & General Trust, which will continue the steam engineering business.

Pontypool & Blaenavon Railway

THE LINE FROM Brynmawr on the LNWR Heads of the Valleys route from Abergavenny to Blaenavon was opened in 1869 by the Brynmawr & Blaenavon Railway and leased to the LNWR. It later joined the GWR giving a route to Newport, which was operated jointly by the GWR and LNWR.

The line closed to passengers as early as 1941 although the section from Blaenavon to Pontypool saw coal traffic from the 'Big Pit' until 1980. North of the main station, Furnace Sidings, the line is the steepest standard gauge preserved passenger-carrying line in Britain. The northern terminus, Whistle Inn Halt, is the highest standard-gauge station in England and Wales.

The Pontypool & Blaenavon Railway was launched in 1980, and started running trains in 1983. In May 2010 the railway opened a 1½-mile extension from Furnace Sidings to Blaenavon High Level, followed in September 2011 with the opening of a further extension to Big Pit Halt, creating a complicated track layout.

Ecclesbourne Valley Railway

LEFT: L&Y 0-6-0 No. 52322 heads a photo charter ballast train away from Duffield on the Ecclesbourne Valley Railway. PHIL WATERFIELD

A VERY LATE starter in heritage railway terms, the nine-mile Duffield to Wirksworth branch in Derbyshire lost its regular passenger services as long ago as 1947. The line was built by the MR envisaging it possibly being part of its Derby to Manchester main line and opening to Wirksworth on October 1, 1867.

The line remained open for limestone traffic from Wirksworth quarries until 1991, after which it was mothballed in case it was ever needed in future. However, a preservation scheme for the Ecclesbourne Valley Railway was launched by WyvernRail in 1996 and Wirksworth station saw its first trains over half a mile of track to Gorsey Bank in 2004, followed by a new line up the 1-in-27 incline to Ravenstor in 2005. Operations were extended southwards and from April 2011 trains ran through to the main line station at Duffield, though there is no physical connection with Network Rail.

Trains are largely DMU-operated but there is an industrial steam presence and there have been occasional main line steam visitors.

Barrow Hill Roundhouse

STAVELEY ROUNDHOUSE was built to a standard Midland Railway locomotive shed design in 1870 and after Nationalisation, became known as Barrow Hill to avoid confusion with the ex-Great Central Staveley shed nearby.

Remarkably, the roundhouse, complete with operational turntable, remained in use by BR for stabling diesel locomotives until as late as February 1991. After final closure, the building was heavily vandalised but was acquired by Chesterfield Borough Council on December 20, 1996 and Grade II listed.

Leased to the Barrow Hill Engine Shed Society, the shed and site has been totally refurbished becoming a major railway heritage site, reopening to the public in July 1998.

It retains its main line connection and has become home to an extensive collection of diesel locomotives as well as a number of steam engines. Occasionally, visiting engines are brought in and line-ups of steam locomotives are staged, including an impressive array of visiting LMS steam power in September 2015.

ABOVE: MR Compound 4-4-0 No. 1000, LMS Ivatt 4MT mogul No. 43106 and MR IF 0-6-0T No. 41708 inside Barrow Hill Roundhouse during the LMS steam gala in September 2015. FRED KERR

RIGHT: LMS 3F 0-6-0T No. 47406, Princess Coronation Pacific No. 46233 *Duchess of Sutherland*, Ivatt 4MT mogul No. 43106 and 'Black Five' 4-6-0 No. 45305 line up at Barrow Hill in September 2015. ROBERT FALCONER

North Norfolk Railway

ANOTHER JOINT LINE the Midland Railway had an interest in was the Midland & Great Northern Joint Railway, although this remained independent after Grouping and became part of the LNER in 1937, never seeing any LMS involvement. BR closed virtually the whole of its extensive system but the North Norfolk Railway now runs trains on the five-mile section from Sheringham to Holt, on which LMS engines feature quite prominently.

Rushden Station

RUSHDEN WAS an intermediate station on the MR's Higham Ferrers branch, opening in 1894, but closing to passengers on June 13, 1959, though freight continued for another 10 years.

The Rushden Historical Transport Society was formed in 1976, and in 1984 the society obtained a lease on the station building, eventually purchasing it 1996.

It has since been restored becoming the Rushden Transport Museum and regularly runs trains over a short length of line with industrial or diesel power.

Midsomer Norton South

THE SOMERSET & Dorset Joint Railway, owned by the MR and the London & South Western Railway, was always popular with enthusiasts and not surprisingly there have been revival schemes though no substantial length of line has been reopened. In the early 1970s a steam centre was established at Radstock, but although brakevan rides were operated, the project ultimately failed, with the Somerset & Dorset Trust relocating to the former GWR West Somerset Railway.

Much more recently, the Somerset & Dorset Railway Heritage Trust aims to restore part of the S&D line from Midsomer Norton to Chilcompton and has operated regular short-distance passenger trains with DMUs or industrial motive power. LMS 'Jinty' 0-6-0T No. 47493 visited in the summer of 2005 but was not able to haul passenger services.

Another separate project has been established further south on the S&D at Shillingstone station. There is also a narrow gauge line south of Templecombe; the Gartell Light Railway, which uses a short section of S&D trackbed, with a planned extension northwards to Templecombe.

Small, but not forgotten...

Narrow gauge or miniature lines that run on one-time LMS routes include the Rudyard Lake Railway on the North Staffordshire line just north of Leek, the Kirklees Light Railway on the L&Y branch to Clayton West and the Leadhills & Wanlockhead Railway on part of a Caledonian Railway branch from Elvanfoot on the main line near Beattock.

Additionally the rebuilt Welsh Highland Railway uses a section of the LNWR branch from Bangor to Afon Wen between its new station at Carnarfon and Dinas Junction.

CHAPTER 2

The National Collection

ABOVE: MR 2-4-0 No. 158A, 4-4-0 No. 1000, 4-2-2 No. 118 and LTSR 4-4-2T No. 80 *Thundersley* at Derby works before being towed to Wirksworth for official photographs in the late 1950s. PB WHITEHOUSE

THE BASIS of the LMS contingent of what became the National Collection has its origins in the presentation by industrial owners of two historic Liverpool & Manchester engines 0-2-2 *Rocket* and 0-4-0 *Sans Pareil* to what would become the Science Museum, for preservation.

The Furness Railway retained its 0-4-0 No. 3 on withdrawal in 1900, while 0-4-2 No. 57 *Lion* became a third L&MR engine to be donated for preservation after industrial service, in early LMS days. The first engine preserved by the LMS on withdrawal was Grand Junction 2-2-2 No. 49 *Columbine*, which was sent to the LNER's railway museum at York in 1926. The LMS also set aside historic LNWR 2-2-2 No. 3020 *Cornwall* for preservation.

The LMS was not one of the best in terms of locomotive preservation. William Stanier is regarded as the man who ordered the scrapping of the GWR's *North Star* and *Lord of the Isles* when he was works manager at Swindon.

And he didn't learn. The LMS had also restored an 1856-built MR 0-6-0 No. 401 in 1929 and North London 4-4-0T No. 6 in NLR livery, and it kept MR 2-4-0 No. 156 and 0-4-4T No. 1226 in 1930, but Stanier came along and had them scrapped in 1932!

But in the 1930s, LNWR 2-4-0 No. 790 *Hardwicke* was retained by Crewe and CR 4-2-2 No. 123 and HR 4-6-0 No. 103 were set aside at St Rollox in view of their historical value. MR 4-2-2 No. 118 had managed to survive Stanier's destruction at Derby and was joined in 1947 by MR 2-4-0 No. 158A.

BR was surprisingly enlightened, even in its early days, MR Compound 4-4-0 No. 1000

was preserved at Derby and L&Y 2-4-2T No. 1008 at Horwich. London Tilbury & Southend Railway 4-4-2T No. 80 *Thundersley* was initially repainted in original livery in 1956 for the centenary of its line and on its retirement immediately afterwards moved to Derby rather than being scrapped.

Then came the list of engines to be preserved, published by the British Transport Commission (BTC) in 1960, which at the time were still in service. These tended to be small,

or goods engines with LMS and pre-Grouping express engines coming out of it badly. No Princess Royal was nominated yet a Princess Coronation was, as Birmingham City Council had announced a serious intention to display No. 46235 *City of Birmingham* on withdrawal.

It took a long time to get LMS engines on permanent public display; there was only Grand Junction Railway No. 49 in York museum until 1961-62 when *Cornwall*, *Hardwicke* and No. 1000 were finally moved

ABOVE: LNWR 2-2-2 No. 3020 in the Museum of British Transport at Clapham in 1973. JOHN TITLOW

into the Museum of British Transport at Clapham. No. 46235 was put on display in the Birmingham Museum of Science and Industry in 1966 and after main line service, the Scottish pair went into Glasgow museum also in 1966. MR Nos. 118 and 158A did find their way into a small museum in Leicester, but the engines withdrawn by BR in the mid- to late 1960s just went into store. Fortunately many were eventually loaned to heritage lines with a view to restoration.

By the end of BR steam in 1968, 23 engines of LMS or its constituents' origins had escaped scrapping and this gave a remarkably representative selection of locomotive types that had worked on the railway. Missing though were most of the company's express 4-4-0s; the LNWR George V and Caledonian Dunalastairs, for example, and the larger pre-Grouping passenger types such as the LNWR Claughton and Caledonian Cardean 4-6-0s, the L&Y 'Highflyer' Atlantics and Dreadnought 4-6-0s.

A GSWR Whitelegg 4-6-4T was an unfortunate omission and we are lucky that just one of this company's steam engines managed to survive in industrial service long enough to be preserved. The missing links, of course, had simply been scrapped or rebuilt long before preservation was taken seriously.

The engines nominated for official preservation towards the end of steam were intended to represent the major designs of the LMS era but, *City of Birmingham* excepted, Stanier was represented by only a three-cylinder 2-6-4T and a 'Black Five' 4-6-0; no Jubilee or rebuilt Royal Scot 4-6-0 was selected nor a Princess Royal Pacific. Fowler was represented by a 4F 0-6-0 and his small contribution to the 'Crab' 2-6-0 but Ivatt was unrepresented, the latter's distinctive moguls in particular being a curious omission, especially as no BR Standard mixed-traffic type was selected either.

ABOVE: Grand Junction Railway 2-2-2 No. 49 *Columbine* in the original York museum in 1972. JOHN TITLOW

The two Scottish veterans, Nos. 103 and 123 had seen main line service from 1959, as had MR No. 1000, but all had retired by 1966. In the 1970s, The Midland Railway Centre at Butterley put 4F 0-6-0 No. 4027 back in steam and Bressingham did the same with Stanier 2-6-2T No. 2500 as well as LTSR 4-4-2T No. 80 *Thundersley*. The National Railway Museum put MR Compound No. 1000 back on the main line and the SVR restored 'Black Five' No. 5000 to main line condition. Butterley also steamed MR Single No. 673 (formerly 118) in 1980. The National Collection's LNWR 0-8-0 No. 49395 remained extremely neglected until much more recently.

Replicas of early locomotives have been built in recent years, the originals having been either scrapped or heavily rebuilt. Working replicas of the Liverpool & Manchester's *Rocket* and *Sans Pareil*, were built for the Rocket 150 celebrations in 1980, while Manchester Museum of Science and Industry built the L&M 2-2-0 No. 9 *Planet*, which has operated at the museum and elsewhere.

Finally, in 1976, the National Collection was able to acquire one of the engines it should have had in the first place, Princess Coronation No. 46229 *Duchess of Hamilton*, and in recent years, the restreamlining of this engine has produced something no-one would ever have expected to see again.

Perhaps even more remarkable is that to date no fewer than 13 of the officially preserved engines have seen active service at some stage, including *Duchess of Hamilton*, though not in its streamlined condition as yet.

BELOW: LNWR 2-4-0 No. 790 *Hardwicke* and MR Compound 4-4-0 No. 1000 depart from Poppleton with a York to Carnforth via Harrogate and Leeds railtour on April 24, 1976.

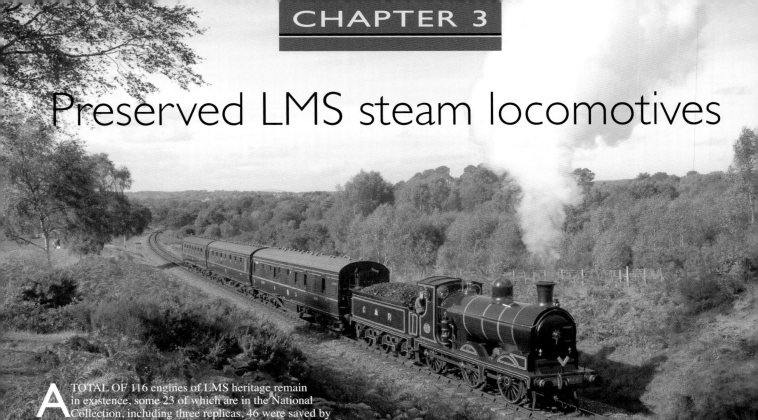

CHAPTER 3

Preserved LMS steam locomotives

A TOTAL OF 116 engines of LMS heritage remain in existence, some 23 of which are in the National Collection, including three replicas, 46 were saved by private preservation and 33 more were purchased from Barry scrapyard after the end of steam.

ABOVE: On a rare visit south of the border, Caledonian Railway 0-6-0 No. 828 approaches Foley Park tunnel on the Severn Valley Railway with a train of LMS stock in October 2011.

Preserved 1825-1922

Type	Number & Name	Built	Preserved	Other No.	Originally	Current location
L&MR 0-2-2	*Rocket*	1829	1862		Kensington	Science Museum
L&MR 0-4-0	*Sans Pareil*	1829	1864		Kensington	Shildon
FR 0-4-0	3 'Coppernob'	1846	1900		Barrow-in-Furness	NRM York
GJR 2-2-2	49 *Columbine*	1846	1902	1868	Crewe	Science Museum

Preserved by the LMS 1923-47

Type	Number & Name	Built	Preserved	Other No.	Originally	Current location
LNWR 2-2-2	3020 *Cornwall*	1858	1925		Crewe	Locomotion
L&MR 0-4-2	57 *Lion*	1838	1928		Liverpool	Liverpool Museum
MR 0-6-0	401	1856	1929		Derby	scrapped
NLR 4-4-0T	6		1929		Derby	scrapped
MR 2-4-0	156		1930		Derby	scrapped
MR 0-4-4T	1226		1930		Derby	scrapped
LNWR 2-4-0	790 *Hardwicke*	1892	1932		Crewe	NRM York
CR 4-2-2	123	1886	1935		St Rollox	Glasgow Mus
HR 4-6-0	103	1896	1934		St Rollox	Glasgow Mus
MR 4-2-2	118	1897	1928	673	Derby	NRM York
MR 2-4-0	158A	1866	1947		Derby	Butterley

Preserved by BR 1948-59

Type	Number & Name	Built	Preserved	Other No.	Originally	Current location
MR 4-4-0	1000	1902	1951	41000	Derby	Barrow Hill
LYR 2-4-2T	1008	1889	1954	50621	Horwich	NRM York
LTSR 4-4-2T	80 *Thundersley*	1909	1956	41946	Derby	Bressingham
HR 4-4-0	54398 *Ben Alder*	1898			Inverness	scrapped

Privately preserved up to 1960

Type	Number & Name	Built	Preserved	Other No.	Originally	Current location
LNWR 0-6-2T	1054	1888	1958	58926	Hednesford	Ingrow
LYR 0-6-0	1300 (as 1122)	1896	1959	52322	Adlington	Ribble
LYR 0-6-0	957	1887	1959	52044	Horwich	KWVR

Nominated for official preservation by the British Transport Commission 1960

Type	Number & Name	Built	Preserved	Other No.	Originally	Current location
LNWR 0-8-0	49395	1921	1961		Stratford	Locomotion
LMS 2-6-4T	42500	1934	1962	2500	Stratford	NRM York
LMS 4-6-2	46235 *City of Birmingham*	1939	1964		Birmingham	Birmingham
LMS 0-6-0	44027	1924	1966	4027	Hellifield	Sharpness
LMS 2-6-0	42700	1926	1966	13000	Hellifield	NRM York
LMS 4-6-0	45000	1935	1967	5000	Hellifield	NRM York

Preserved privately 1961-66

Type	Number & Name	Built	Preserved	Other No.	Originally	Current location
NLR 0-6-0T	58850	1880	1960	2650	Bluebell	Bluebell
CR 0-4-4T	55189	1907	1963	419	Falkirk	Bo'nes
LMS 4-6-0	46100 *Royal Scot*	1927	1963	6100	Skegness	Crewe
LMS 4-6-2	46201 *Princess Elizabeth*	1933	1963	6201	Ashchurch	Tyseley
LMS 4-6-2	46203 *Princess Margaret Rose*	1935	1963		Pwllheli	Butterley
LMS 4-6-2	46229 *Duchess of Hamilton*	1938	1964	6229	Minehead	NRM York
LMS 4-6-2	46233 *Duchess of Sutherland*	1938	1964	46233	Ayr	Butterley
LYR 0-4-0ST	51218	1901	1965	68	KWVR	KWVR
CR 0-6-0	57566	1899	1966	828	Glasgow Mus	Strathspey
LMS 4-6-0	45596 *Bahamas*	1935	1966	5596	Dinting	Tyseley
LMS 4-6-0	46115 *Scots Guardsman*	1927	1966	6115	KWVR	Carnforth

Private preservation filled many gaps left in the collection of officially preserved locomotives. In particular we have the unique survivor from the North London Railway, an L&Y 'Pug' 0-4-0ST, Stanier Jubilee and Royal Scot 4-6-0s, and a Princess Royal Pacific.

Preserved privately 1967-72

MR 0-6-0T	41708	1880	1967	1708	KWVR	Barrow Hill
LMS 2-6-2T	41241	1949	1967		KWVR	KWVR
LMS 2-6-2T	41298	1951	1967		Longmoor	Isle of Wight
LMS 2-6-0	46441	1950	1967	6441	Carnforth	Ribble
LMS 2-6-0	46443	1950	1967		SVR	SVR
LMS 2-6-0	46464	1950	1967		Dundee	Brechin
LMS 2-6-4T	42073	1950	1968	2073	Carnforth	Lakeside
LMS 2-6-4T	42085	1950	1968	2085	Carnforth	Lakeside
LMS 0-6-0T	47383	1926	1968		SVR	SVR
LMS 4-6-0	45593 *Kolhapur*	1935	1967	5593	Tyseley	Tyseley
LMS 2-6-0	43106	1951	1968		SVR	SVR
LMS 2-8-0	48773	1940	1968	8233	Tyseley	SVR
LMS 0-6-0T	47564	1928	1972		Derby	Butterley

By 1967, there was only a limited number of classes left working for BR. Nevertheless, private preservation still filled some gaps as the end of BR steam drew near, including an 8F 2-8-0 plus Fairburn 4MT 2-6-4Ts and Ivatt 2-6-2Ts, 2MT moguls and a 4MT mogul.

'Black Fives' preserved 1967-69

Type	Number & Name	Built	Preserved	Other No.	Originally	Current location
LMS 4-6-0	44767	1947	1969	4767 'George Stephenson'	Carnforth	Butterley
LMS 4-6-0	44806	1944	1969	4806 'Magpie'	Carnforth	NYMR
LMS 4-6-0	44871	1945	1968	'Sovereign'	Carnforth	Rileys
LMS 4-6-0	44932	1945	1969		Carnforth	Carnforth
LMS 4-6-0	45025	1934	1969	5025	KWVR	Strathspey
LMS 4-6-0	45110	1935	1969	'RAF Biggin Hill'	Ashford	Severn Valley
LMS 4-6-0	45212	1935	1968		KWVR	Rileys
LMS 4-6-0	45231	1936	1968	5231 'The Sherwood Forester'	Carnforth	Carnforth
LMS 4-6-0	45305	1936	1969	5305 'Alderman AE Draper'	Hull	GCR
LMS 4-6-0	45407	1937	1968	5407 'The Glasgow Highlander'	Carnforth	Rileys
LMS 4-6-0	45428	1937	1967	5428 'Eric Treacy'	Holbeck	NYMR

Stanier's popular and numerous 'Black Five' 4-6-0s were the engines that largely brought the BR steam era to a close. Any budding locomotive owner was running out of time in 1968 and after August 11, there was something of a rush to acquire 'Black Fives' for preservation, resulting in the class remaining one of the most numerous in the preservation era, just as it was in steam days.

Preserved after industrial service

Type	Number & Name	Built	Preserved	Originally	Current location
LNWR 0-4-0ST	1439	1865	1954	Crewe	Ribble
Mersey 0-6-4T	5 *Cecil Raikes*	1886	1956	Derby	Liverpool
FR 0-4-0	17	1865	1960	Ulverston	Carnforth
FR 0-4-0	20	1863	1960	Barrow	Locomotion
GSWR 0-6-0T	9	1917	1965	Glasgow Mus	Glasgow Mus
NSR 0-6-2T	2	1923	1966	Shugborough	Locomotion
LYR 0-4-0ST	11243	1910	1967	KWVR	Ribble
LYR 0-6-0ST	752	1881	1968	Heywood	KWVR
LMS 0-6-0T	47445	1927	1970	Derby	Butterley

The survival of one-time LMS constituents' locomotives in industrial service has led to the preservation of several fascinating survivors including unique locomotives from the Mersey and North Staffordshire Railways. Two ancient Furness Railway 0-4-0s converted to saddletanks survived and one has even been back-converted to original condition and returned to steam.

Purchased from Barry scrapyard

Type	Number & Name	Built	Preserved	Other No.	Originally	Current location
MR 0-6-0	43924	1920	1968	3924	KWVR	KWVR
LMS 0-6-0T	47327	1926	1970	23	Derby	Butterley
LMS 0-6-0T	47357	1926	1970	16440	Derby	Butterley
SDJR 2-8-0	53808	1925	1970	88	Radstock	W Somerset
LMS 2-6-0	46521	1953	1971		SVR	GCR
LMS 4-6-0	45690 *Leander*	1936	1972	5690	Dinting	Carnforth
LMS 0-6-0T	47493	1927	1972		East Somerset	Spa Valley
LMS 2-6-0	46447	1950	1972		Quainton Road	E Somerset
LMS 2-8-0	48431	1944	1972	8431	KWVR	KWVR
LMS 2-6-0	46512	1953	1973		Hereford	Strathspey
LMS 2-6-0	42968	1934	1973		SVR	SVR
LMS 4-6-0	45379	1937	1974		Bitton	Mid Hants
LMS 0-6-0T	47298	1924	1974	7298	Southport	Llangollen
LMS 2-6-2T	41312	1952	1974		Caerphilly	Mid Hants
LMS 2-6-2T	41313	1952	1975		Quainton Road	E Somerset
LMS 2-8-0	48151	1942	1975		Embsay	Carnforth
SDJR 2-8-0	53809	1925	1975	13809	Kirk Smeaton	Butterley
LMS 0-6-0	44422	1927	1977	4422	Cheddleton	W Somerset
LMS 2-6-0	42765	1927	1978	13065	KWVR	ELR
LMS 0-6-0T	47324	1926	1978		Mid-Hants	ELR
LMS 2-6-0	46428	1948	1979		Strathspey	ELR
LMS 0-6-0T	47279	1924	1979		KWVR	KWVR
LMS 4-6-0	45699 *Galatea*	1936	1980		Carnforth	Carnforth
LMS 0-6-0	44123	1925	1981		Mid Hants	Bitton
LMS 4-6-0	45491	1943	1981		Fleetwood	Butterley
LMS 2-8-0	48624	1943	1981	8624	Buxton	GCR
LMS 0-6-0T	47406	1926	1983		Buxton	GCR
LMS 4-6-0	45337	1937	1984	M5337	ELR	NVR
LMS 2-8-0	48305	1943	1985		GCR	GCR
LMS 4-6-0	45293	1936	1986		North Woolwich	Castle Hed.
LMS 2-6-0	42859	1930	1986		Hull	Private location
LMS 4-6-0	45163	1935	1987		Hull	Castle Hed.
LMS 4-6-0	44901	1945	1988		Bute Street	Sharpness
LMS 2-8-0	48173	1943	1988		Bitton	Churnet
LMS 2-8-0	48518	1944	1988		Bute Street	scrap

The presence of a considerable number of LMS engines in the scrapyard at Barry in South Wales led to a considerable increase in the overall total of the company's engines in preservation, although unfortunately as they were late survivors in BR days, they all virtually duplicated existing types in existence. Nevertheless it has led to the active preservation of two of the popular and distinctive Somerset & Dorset 7F 2-8-0s and has added to the stock of useful engines on our heritage lines. Several still remain unrestored

RIGHT: LMS Princess Coronation Pacific No. 6229 *Duchess of Hamilton* at Butlin's holiday camp at Minehead. COLOUR-RAIL.COM

BELOW: L&M 0-4-2 *Lion* passes Burscough Bridge en route from Steamport Southport to the Rocket 150 celebrations at Rainhill on May 18, 1980.

From overseas

Type	Number & Name	Built	Preserved	Other No.	Originally	Current location
TCDD 2-8-0	45160	1940	1989	8274	Swanage	Ruddington
TCDD 2-8-0	45166	1940	2010		Barry	Bo'ness
TCDD 2-8-0	45170	1940	2010	70414	Hepscott	Israel

The survival of a handful of LMS 8F 2-8-0s in Turkey, where they worked until the 1970s was not initially of interest to preservationists, in view of their remoteness and poor condition. But the Turks did not scrap them and eventually when it looked as if it might be possible to move them, one was repatriated and then later two more. There are still other possibilities; another 8F survives in Baghdad, and a Mersey Railway 0-6-4T is preserved, though derelict, in Australia.

New build

LMR 0-2-2	*Rocket*	1980	NRM York
LMR 0-4-0	*Sans Pareil*	1980	Locomotion
LMR 2-2-0	*Planet*	1992	Manchester
LNWR 2-2-2	1009 *Wolverton*	1991	Wolverton
LNWR 2-2-2	'Bloomer 2'		Tyseley
LMS 4-6-0	45551 *The Unknown Warrior*		Llangollen

Working replicas of *Rocket* and *Sans Pareil* were built for the Liverpool & Manchester 150th anniversary celebrations in 1980, and another L&MR engine was built in 1992. An LNWR 'Bloomer' was built, not to be operational, although another member of the class is under construction as a working replica. However the major 'new-build' project is the construction of an unrebuilt LMS Patriot 4-6-0, which will fill a big gap in the stock of preserved LMS engines

CHAPTER 4

LMS steam on the main line

ABOVE: LMS Jubilee 4-6-0 No. 45690 *Leander* tackles the southbound climb to Shap on the electrified West Coast Main Line at Little Strickland with Vintage Trains' 'Cumbrian Jubilee' on March 21, 2015, using the company's own coaching stock, operated by West Coast Railways.

THE LMS DID not quite make the same contribution to steam preservation as, for example the LNER, which staged the 1925 Stockton & Darlington Railway centenary followed by the opening of a railway museum at York. The LNER also brought the Stirling Single GNR No. 1 out of the museum in 1938 for publicity purposes and even used it on public excursions. The only significant venture into the operation of preserved steam by the LMS was to steam L&MR 0-4-2 *Lion* in 1930 and run it alongside the 'Coronation Scot' on the WCML in 1938.

Similarly after Nationalisation, while the GN Atlantics came out of retirement on the Eastern Region in the early 1950s, the LMR did not get involved. In 1956 though, to

BELOW: The first LMS Pacific to haul a main line passenger train in preservation, LMS Princess Royal Pacific No. 6201 *Princess Elizabeth* tackles Gresford bank near Wrexham with its second railtour on June 5, 1976.

celebrate the centenary of the LT&SR, 4-4-2T No. 41946 did get restored to original livery as No. 80 *Thundersley* for the line's centenary and the repaint was to result in the engine being retained for preservation.

More significantly though, the Scottish Region returned four preserved veterans to steam in 1959, two of which had originally been set aside by the LMS in the mid-1930s and at the same time the LMR steamed the Midland Compound No. 1000 and put it to work on excursions for a couple of years.

As private steam preservation gained momentum in the mid-1960s, the former LNER remained at the forefront with A3 Pacific No. 4472 *Flying Scotsman* plus three A4 Pacifics and K4 2-6-0 No. 3442 *The Great Marquess* seeing action, while the GWR saw

two preserved Castle 4-6-0s and other engines in active main line service. Although big LMS main line engines were purchased privately for preservation, none came close to hauling a main line passenger train in the 1960s, however, LMS Pacific No. 6201 *Princess Elizabeth* made a couple of overnight light engine runs. It all ended in October 1967 when BR introduced a ban on all operations of privately owned steam engines on its tracks. Yet by this time the LMR was the only region still operating its own steam engines, mostly of LMS origin and this continued until August 1968, the end of main line steam, with the exception of *Flying Scotsman*, which soldiered on for 12 months before embarking on a tour of North America.

STEAM BAN LIFTED

The BR ban was lifted in 1972 and a very limited series of steam excursions was allowed on selected routes by 'approved' locomotives. Two or three 'Black Five' 4-6-0s saw action on the Cumbrian Coast while Jubilee No. 5596 *Bahamas* ran on the Hope Valley and the Welsh borders. Gradually, the 'approved' routes were extended and further engines were added to the 'approved' list, although for a long time Britain's main lines were still not graced by any of the LMS Class 7s or Class 8s.

In 1975 came the Stockton & Darlington 150th anniversary and, as in 1925, the celebrations featured engines from the other railways as well as the LNER. This would be followed by the opening of a new museum at York and LMS main line preserved steam benefited significantly.

No. 6201 *Princess Elizabeth* made the long journey from Ashchurch to the North East light engine, but returned doubleheaded with SR Merchant Navy Pacific No. 35028 *Clan Line* on a four-coach train. The stage was set in 1976 for an LMS Pacific to take to the main line once again at the head of a passenger train. More surprising though was that when the collection of preserved locomotives was removed from Clapham museum and mostly relocated to York, certain engines were selected for steaming at the Shildon cavalcade, with LNWR Precedent 2-4-0 No. 790 *Hardwicke* being handled at Carnforth, while MR Compound 4-4-0 No. 1000 was dealt with at York. Both duly steamed to Shildon in 1975 and the following year commenced a short period of main line excursion service, initially doubleheading from York to Carnforth in April.

SETTLE & CARLISLE

1978 saw a significant development when the Settle & Carlisle line was cleared for steam operations but LMS power was in short supply to begin with. The same year also saw BR commence its own steam operations, initially using LNER Pacifics running two days a week on the Cumbrian Coast line, as well as York-Scarborough excursions, programmes that were expanded and would later feature LMS motive power. The SLOA Marketing 'Cumbrian Mountain Express' programme was launched in 1980 and saw fairly regular Settle & Carlisle steam.

The three Carnforth 'Black Fives' were joined by two more main line certified members of the class; No. 4767 *George Stephenson* in 1976 and No. 5305 *Alderman AE Draper* in 1977. Another 'Black Five', the National Collection's No. 5000 was returned to the main line in 1979 and this was the start of a serious involvement in main line steam running by the Severn Valley Railway, being followed in 1980 by Ivatt 4MT mogul No. 43106 and in subsequent years by 8F No. 8233, Ivatt 2MT No. 46521, Stanier mogul No. 2968, and 'Black Five' No. 45110, along with many GWR and BR Standard designs.

These smaller engines proved popular and the SVR even purchased something bigger, Jubilee No. 5690 *Leander*, specifically as a main line flagship, but eventually it was decided that the SVR needed to concentrate on its own railway and its main line running was phased out.

The welcome return of a Royal Scot to the main line came in 1978 in the shape of No. 6115 *Scots Guardsman* but its career was shortlived. Far more significant was the 1980 debut of No. 46229 *Duchess of Hamilton*, arguably the most popular of all preserved

main line steam engines.

The Liverpool & Manchester 150th anniversary cavalcade at Rainhill in 1980 had provided the incentive to get many LMS engines back in steam. L&M 0-4-2 *Lion*, MR Johnson Single No. 673, and 4F 0-6-0 No. 4027 made their way to Lancashire under their own steam although this was not a prelude to any main line passenger working. However, LNWR Webb Coal Tank No. 1054 did haul short trips out of Manchester Victoria during the summer of 1984, and in 1981, Somerset & Dorset 7F 2-8-0 No. 13809 made its preserved main line passenger debut, even reaching York on the ECML.

The LMS routes in Scotland saw little steam action in the 1970s although approval had been given for Strathspey's 'Black Five' No. 5025 to run to Kyle of Lochalsh. When the Highland main line was cleared for steam excursions, it was an LNER A4 Pacific that got the ball rolling but No. 5025 soon followed and made it to the Kyle a couple of times in 1982.

In 1987, *Flying Scotsman* was booked for a

> The three Carnforth 'Black Fives' were joined by two more main line members of the class...

trip from Derby to Buxton, the first steam train to the town for 20 years, but failed and the substitute engine, newly restored 8F 2-8-0 No. 48151 was not only much more appropriate for the route through Peak Forest but was to start a revolution in main line steam operation, being owned by Yorkshire businessman David Smith.

Two red engines took to the main line in 1990, Dr Beet's Ivatt mogul No. 46441 and Brell Ewart's No. 46203 *Princess Margaret Rose*, but change was coming to the railways in the shape of privatisation.

This had two significant repercussions. Firstly, there was 'open access'. Anyone could set up a Train Operating Company and within reason, run trains anywhere; it would no longer be possible for steam to be restricted to certain routes as had been the case under BR. Secondly this gave the opportunity for TOCs to be set up primarily to run steam and two such

organisations came into being. Pop impresario Pete Waterman purchased the InterCity Special Trains Unit from BR, while David Smith acquired the Steamtown centre at Carnforth and set up West Coast Railways.

TAKING ADVANTAGE

The railtour establishment; the tour promoters as opposed to operators, were slow to react and it was a newcomer, Mel Chamberlin of Days Out Ltd, who really took full advantage of 'open access' and among other things, brought steam back to Shap and Euston. The more established tour companies had to follow and we saw steam return to the Lickey incline in the mid-1990s.

Duchess of Hamilton suddenly had the opportunity to show what it could do on its home turf and some memorable runs followed, including a final run from Euston to Glasgow in 1998, before its return to York and static preservation. However, Brell Ewart's Princess Margaret Rose Locomotive Trust had managed to obtain the other one-time Butlin's Duchess, No. 6233 *Duchess of Sutherland* and returned it to steam in 2000. *Hamilton*'s would be a hard act to follow but *Sutherland* received the ultimate accolade in 2002 when it was chosen to haul the Royal Train along the North Wales coast line.

Mel Chamberlin's venture into main line steam running was spectacular but shortlived, and Waterman Railways similarly faded away. Main line steam operations on the privatised railway system were handled by freight company English Welsh & Scottish Railways, but West Coast Railways had mounted a successful challenge to what appeared to be a monopoly situation and having become a TOC in its own right has since built up its business to become the dominant main line steam operator in Britain. It has since ensured that big LMS steam power can be enjoyed, on the Settle & Carlisle especially, several times a week during the summer months; active engines now on its books having been supplemented by Jubilee No. 45699 *Galatea* and Royal Scot No. 46115 *Scots Guardsman*.

A significant return to the main line is expected in February 2016 when the other preserved 'Scot', No. 46100 *Royal Scot* itself finally returns to main line service, having been one of the first LMS express engines to enter private preservation, way back in the early 1960s.

BELOW: Hauling the fortunately shortlived 'Pilkington' green set of coaches, LMS 'Black Five' 4-6-0 No. 44767 *George Stephenson* passes Thornhill on the Calder Valley line with Days Out Ltd's first railtour, from Darlington to Manchester, on March 18, 1995.

CHAPTER 5

Liverpool and Manchester Railway

THE LIVERPOOL & MANCHESTER was Britain's first public inter-city passenger railway. It opened in 1830, five years after the Stockton & Darlington Railway, and was again engineered by George Stephenson. Its route still forms the principal link between the two cities today, out of which grew the London & North Western Railway and eventually the London Midland & Scottish Railway.

0-2-2 Rocket

STEPHENSON'S *ROCKET* was built in 1829 at the Forth Street works of Robert Stephenson and Company in Newcastle-upon-Tyne. At the time that it was designed, George Stephenson was overseeing the building of the L&MR, and his son Robert was in charge of designing and constructing the locomotive.

As is well-known, *Rocket* won the Rainhill Trials, held by the Liverpool & Manchester Railway in 1829 to choose the best design of steam locomotive for the railway. It combined several innovations to produce the most advanced locomotive of its day, and was an important stage in an evolving design of Stephenson's locomotives that set the pattern for most steam locomotives in the following 150 years.

Rocket had a tall chimney at the front with a blastpipe, and a multi-tube boiler with a separate firebox. The large single pair of wooden wheels was driven directly by two external cylinders set at an angle, producing for the first time a fast, light locomotive but of only moderate power, in other words an engine

built for passenger trains.

Rocket was later rebuilt so that the cylinders were set close to horizontal, which was to become standard for nearly all subsequent steam designs.

The design was rapidly developed and enlarged after the railway opened for business and by as early as 1836, *Rocket* was seen as underpowered and so was sold for £300 to work on a mineral line near Brampton in Cumberland where it worked until 1862.

In that year, *Rocket* was donated by its owners to the Patent Office Museum in London, later to become the Science Museum. It remains on display in this museum, although in much modified condition.

RIGHT: The original *Rocket* on display in the Science Museum in Kensington. ROBIN JONES

BELOW: A working replica of *Rocket* was built in 1980. It took part in the Liverpool & Manchester Railway 150th anniversary cavalcade at Rainhill on May 25, 1980.

LMR 0-4-0 *Sans Pareil*

ROCKET'S main competitor at the Rainhill trials was 0-4-0 *Sans Pareil* built by Timothy Hackworth. It was somewhat antiquated in comparison with *Rocket*, having a boiler with a double return flue and with the firebox and chimney both positioned at the rear.

It had two cylinders, mounted vertically at the opposite end to the chimney, and driving one pair of driving wheels directly, with the other pair being driven by connecting rods.

In any case it slightly exceeded the maximum weight permitted for the trials and was hopelessly uneconomic, and a cracked cylinder soon put it out of the competition. The railway still bought *Sans Pareil* but it was leased to the Bolton and Leigh Railway where it ran until 1844. It was then used as a stationary boiler at Coppull Colliery, Chorley until 1863, after which it was restored, and like *Rocket*, presented to the Patent Office Museum in 1864 by John Hick.

It is now displayed in the Hackworth Museum at Shildon, where it was built, close to the new Locomotion Museum.

FAR RIGHT: The original L&M 0-4-0 *Sans Pareil* on display in the Hackworth Museum at Shildon.

ABOVE: *Sans Pareil* and L&MR 0-4-2 *Lion* in the Rainhill cavalcade on May 25, 1980.

0-4-2 No. 57 *Lion*

NO. 57 *LION* was one of a pair of 0-4-2s designed for L&MR goods traffic, by Todd, Kitson & Laird (later Kitsons) of Leeds in 1838. *Lion* received a new boiler in around 1845 and ran until about 1858.

The following year it was sold to the Mersey Docks and Harbour Board for use as a stationary engine where it was used until as late as 1928 when it was replaced by an electric pump. It was discovered, and the Old Locomotive Committee was set up, which arranged for it to be overhauled at Crewe.

Lion was returned to steam and took part in the L&MR centenary celebrations in 1930, running round a circular track in Wavertree Park in Liverpool. It was put on a plinth at Lime Street station in 1931 but steamed again for the London and Birmingham Railway centenary in 1938 when it ran alongside the 'Coronation Scot'.

A surprisingly active survivor, it famously starred in the 1953 film The Titfield Thunderbolt, and others, but in 1979, it was moved to the English Electric (former Vulcan Foundry) works at Newton-le-Willows for a major overhaul before taking part in the 1980 L&MR Rocket 150 celebrations at Rainhill, site of the 1829 trials.

Amazingly, on March 18, 1980 it ran under its own steam from the Steamport museum at Southport, to Bold Colliery near St Helens, hauling two replica L&MR four-wheeled coaches, even running on a short section of the electrified WCML.

Lion saw service at other railway centres for a while but returned to store in Liverpool in 1982, before moving to Liverpool Road station in Manchester in June 1999, where the original L&MR station had been converted to the Manchester Museum of Science and Industry.

On February 27, 2007 though, *Lion* was moved by road from Manchester to Liverpool for cosmetic restoration work before resuming life as a static exhibit, now in the transport gallery of the new Museum of Liverpool.

ABOVE LEFT: *Lion* and LMS *Princess Coronation Pacific* No. 6225 *Duchess of Gloucester* on display at Euston in September 1938.

ABOVE RIGHT: *Lion* on display in the Musueum of Liverpool. ROBIN JONES

ABOVE: The unprecedented sight of *Lion* on the electrified West Coast Main Line at Golborne on May 18, 1980.

LMR 2-2-0
No. 9 *Planet*

NO. 9 *PLANET* was constructed in 1830 for the L&MR; the railway's ninth locomotive. It represented Stephenson's next major development of the *Rocket*, being the first locomotive with inside cylinders. As early as November 1830, *Planet* completed the journey from Liverpool to Manchester in an hour.

A replica was built by the Friends of the Museum of Science and Industry in 1992 and has been used to give short steam train rides at the museum in Manchester, as well as making occasional appearances elsewhere.

RIGHT: The replica L&MR 2-2-0 *Planet* at Liverpool Road. ROBIN JONES

Grand Junction Railway

THE FIRST PART of the Grand Junction Railway was opened in 1837 and merged with the Liverpool and Manchester Railway in 1845. The following year it amalgamated with the London and Birmingham Railway and Manchester and Birmingham Railway to form the London and North Western Railway.

It was the first long-distance steam-worked trunk railway in the world, and now forms the central section of the West Coast Main Line.

Engineered by George Stephenson and Joseph Locke, the 82-mile line ran from Birmingham to Warrington, then via the existing Warrington and Newton Railway to

join the Liverpool and Manchester Railway. The GJR moved its main engineering works from Edge Hill in Liverpool to Crewe in 1843.

The GJR later shared Curzon Street station in Birmingham with the London and Birmingham Railway providing a link from London to Liverpool and Manchester.

2-2-2 No. 49
Columbine

THE GJR BUILT *COLUMBINE* at Crewe in 1845. It was a 2-2-2 designed by Francis Trevithick and Alexander Allan. Known as the 'Crewe type' with outside cylinders and a double frame, such engines were popular right across Europe in their day. *Columbine* was a typical express passenger engine of the time and few locomotives from this era have survived.

It was renumbered 1868 by the LNWR after 1846, and worked until 1902, when it was put to one side in Crewe works by the LNWR, possibly as it was believed, incorrectly, to have been the first engine ever built at Crewe. It was sent to the LNER's new railway museum at York on its opening in 1926 where it remained on display until moved to the National Railway Museum in the city during November 1974 in readiness for its opening in September 1975. However, September 26, 1999 saw it transferred to the Science Museum in London where it is on show in LNWR black livery.

LEFT: GJR No. 49 *Columbine*, as LNWR No. 1868 on display in the Science Museum. ROBIN JONES

Simplified map of the London Midland & Scottish Railway showing constituent companies

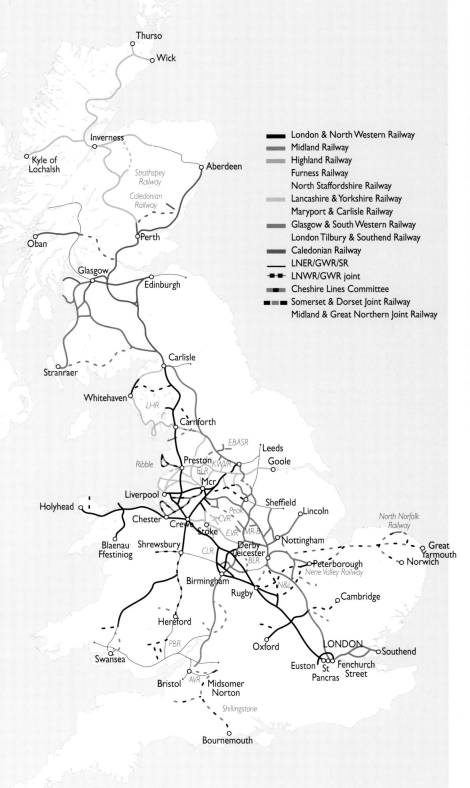

Legend:

- London & North Western Railway
- Midland Railway
- Highland Railway
- Furness Railway
- North Staffordshire Railway
- Lancashire & Yorkshire Railway
- Maryport & Carlisle Railway
- Glasgow & South Western Railway
- London Tilbury & Southend Railway
- Caledonian Railway
- LNER/GWR/SR
- LNWR/GWR joint
- Cheshire Lines Committee
- Somerset & Dorset Joint Railway
- Midland & Great Northern Joint Railway

Locations:

Thurso, Wick, Inverness, Kyle of Lochalsh, Aberdeen, *Strathspey Railway*, *Caledonian Railway*, Oban, Perth, Glasgow, Edinburgh, Stranraer, Carlisle, Whitehaven, *LHR*, Carnforth, *EBASR*, Leeds, Goole, *Ribble*, Preston, *ELR*, *KWVR*, Mcr, Liverpool, Sheffield, Lincoln, Holyhead, Chester, Crewe, Stoke, *Peak*, *CVR*, *EVR*, *MR-B*, Nottingham, *North Norfolk Railway*, Blaenau Ffestiniog, Shrewsbury, *CLR*, Derby, Leicester, *BLR*, Peterborough, *Nene Valley Railway*, Great Yarmouth, Norwich, Birmingham, *N&I*, Cambridge, Rugby, Hereford, *PBR*, Oxford, LONDON, Southend, Swansea, Euston, St Pancras, Fenchurch Street, *AVR*, Bristol, Midsomer Norton, *Shillingstone*, Bournemouth

ABOVE: No. 790 *Hardwicke* hauls three LNWR Royal Train coaches in the Rocket 150 cavalcade at Rainhill on the original Liverpool and Manchester Railway on May 25, 1980.

London and North Western Railway

THE LONDON Western Railway became one of Britain's biggest independent railway companies and, of course, could trace its origins back to the Liverpool & Manchester Railway. In the late 19th century the LNWR was the largest joint stock company in the world; at its peak it had a route mileage of more than 1500 miles and employed 111,000 people.

The LNWR described itself as the Premier Line, and its system was based around the West Coast Main Line from Euston to Carlisle. Other major routes were from Crewe to Holyhead, the main connection to Ireland, and from Liverpool to Manchester and Leeds. Numerous acquisitions of smaller companies eventually saw its territory extending to Derby, Nottingham, Cambridge and South Wales.

The LNWR inherited the locomotive works at Crewe from the Grand Junction Railway and this became one of the most respected locomotive building works in the country.

Locomotives were painted green at first,

but from 1873 black, often described as 'blackberry black' became the standard livery, and this livery with red, cream and grey lining was much later adopted by BR as its standard livery for mixed-traffic locomotives.

It expanded further by merging with the Lancashire & Yorkshire Railway in 1922, shortly before Grouping, which saw it become a major part of the London Midland & Scottish Railway.

Some LNWR routes were closed by BR in the 1960s, notably Peterborough to Northampton, Cambridge to Oxford, Penrith to Workington and the Heads of the Valleys line, but its system has remained largely

intact, serving some of Britain's most densely populated areas.

The main heritage line on the one-time LNWR is the Nene Valley Railway which operates 7½ miles of the former Peterborough to Northampton and Rugby line based at Wansford. The Battlefield Line in Leicestershire uses part of a LNWR/Midland joint line and the Northampton & Lamport Railway runs trains on a short section of the Northampton to Market Harborough line. A very short section of LNWR trackbed now carries the 1ft 11½in gauge Welsh Highland Railway through Carnarfon.

Five very different LNWR steam locomotives survive in preservation, ranging from an ancient Ramsbottom 0-4-0ST to the historic single-wheeler *Cornwall* and the long-lived heavy freight 'Super D' 0-8-0. Sadly though, none of the oddities such as the Compound 2-2-2-2s survive, neither do the later express types such as the George V 4-4-0s or Claughton 4-6-0s.

ABOVE: LNWR-2-2-2 No. 3020 *Cornwall* stands outside the Locomotion museum at Shildon.

2-2-2 No. 3020 *Cornwall*

NO. 173 *CORNWALL* was built at Crewe works in 1847 as a 4-2-2 and was designed by Francis Trevithick, the son of Cornish steam pioneer Richard Trevithick. He was the resident engineer, then locomotive superintendent of the Grand Junction Railway, which became the LNWR.

In the 1840s, eight foot or more diameter driving wheels were standard for express passenger engines. The original design of *Cornwall* with its 8ft 6in single driving wheels, had its boiler under the driving axle and the trailing axle in a tube through the firebox and was shown at the 1851 Great Exhibition.

Needless to say it was soon extensively rebuilt under the LNWR's engineer Ramsbottom, and became a more conventional 2-2-2 in 1858.

A less drastic rebuild in the 1870s saw *Cornwall* acquire a typical LNWR cab, and it was allocated a new number, 3020, in June 1886.

Cornwall was a very successful express engine, and known to have achieved 70mph down Whitmore bank near Crewe in 1884. It was withdrawn from express service on the Liverpool-Manchester route in 1902 but was then used to haul the mechanical engineer's inspection coach into early LMS days.

In view of its longevity *Cornwall* was

preserved by the LMS, and normally retained at Crewe works, although occasionally exhibited in public, such as in 1938 for the centenary of the London & Birmingham Railway.

It was finally put on permanent exhibition in the Museum of British Transport at Clapham on December 16, 1962, but on closure of the museum, returned to Crewe works in 1975. It spent a period on loan to the Severn Valley Railway as a static exhibit from August 16, 1979 to September 15, 1983 when it finally made it to the National Railway Museum at York. It is currently on display at the Locomotion museum in Shildon.

0-4-0ST No. 1439

ABOVE: LNWR 0-4-0ST No. 1439 on display at the Ribble Steam Railway at Preston.

IN 1839 JOHN RAMSBOTTOM joined Sharp, Roberts and Company of Manchester, builders of stationary engines and steam locomotives. He became locomotive superintendent of the Manchester and Birmingham Railway in 1842, which in 1846 became part of the LNWR, where Ramsbottom became district superintendent, North Eastern Division. In 1857 Ramsbottom became locomotive superintendent of the Northern Division, based at Crewe. He is credited with designing and introducing the first water troughs.

0-4-0ST No. 1439 was built at Crewe in 1865. It was rebuilt in November 1887 and again in September 1898, and the original Ramsbottom chimney would have been replaced by a Webb pattern at one of these rebuildings, and a cab added. It worked for a period in and around Liverpool docks. It was loaned to Kynoch Ltd, at Witton, Birmingham in 1914, subsequently being purchased five years later, becoming its No. 4.

A new boiler was supplied by Bagnall in 1935, at an increased pressure of 160psi. The boiler has a cylindrical steel firebox; unusual in a steam locomotive. The Ramsbottom smokebox, with flap door, survived the rebuildings.

The engine worked until as late as 1953 and was given by Kynoch's successors, ICI, to the BTC in 1954; a welcome addition to steam preservation as the only remaining locomotive of the Ramsbottom era. It was stored for a while at Hellifield, before being put on display at Shugborough Hall in Staffordshire in 1967. It has moved since, to the Severn Valley Railway in 1983-84, and to the NRM in September 1985. It joined the collection on the Ribble Steam Railway in Preston during January 2009, and is now on display in the museum building. It has never steamed in preservation.

Also dating from the Ramsbottom era is the diminutive 18in gauge Crewe works shunter *Pet*, built in 1865, withdrawn in 1929 and preserved at the NRM.

BELOW: On its last main line passenger run, No. 790 *Hardwicke* and BR Standard 9F 2-10-0 No. 92220 *Evening Star* depart from Long Preston on June 19, 1976.

Webb Precedent 2-4-0 No. 790 *Hardwicke*

FRANCIS WILLIAM WEBB, who took over from Ramsbottom as the LNWR's chief mechanical engineer in 1871, became one of Britain's best-known 19th-century locomotive engineers. In 1851 at the age of 15 he was articled as a pupil of Francis Trevithick at Crewe, rising to works manager by 1861 under Ramsbottom. After a period at a steelmakers in Bolton, in October 1870, Webb was appointed as LNWR locomotive superintendent, and soon redesignated chief mechanical engineer.

Webb introduced some very successful standard locomotive classes, large numbers of which were built at Crewe. A Precedent 2-4-0 and a Coal Tank 0-6-2T survive but the Coal Engine and 'Cauliflower' 0-6-0s were all scrapped. Webb introduced the heavy freight 0-8-0 to the LNWR and these were continuously developed and built into LMS days, some running until the mid-1960s. One of the final developments of the 0-8-0s is preserved.

MISPLACED FAITH

However, it was not all good. Webb used two varieties of compounding in a number of his locomotive designs, which gave a lot of trouble as the high- and low-pressure cylinders drove separate axles with no coupling rods. He is remembered for having somewhat misplaced faith in this design to the bemusement of his contemporaries.

Webb was also responsible for the remodelling of Crewe station, which involved four track underpasses to keep freight traffic out of the way of passenger trains.

Webb designed the 'Improved' or 'Renewed' Precedent express 2-4-0 and 160

were built at Crewe between 1887 and 1902. They were officially 'renewals' of the original Precedents and some 'Newtons' for accounting purposes, although eight Precedents were not renewed. The 'new' engines retained their names and already haphazard numbers, and eventually acquired the nickname 'Jumbos'.

They were extremely effective engines for their time and one member of the class, No. 790 *Hardwicke*, covered the 141-mile Crewe-Carlisle stage of the 1895 West Coast v East Coast Race to the North on August 22, 1895, in just two hours six minutes at an average speed of 67.1mph. This set a record time for the route that has never been bettered by steam.

Withdrawals started in December 1905, but 76 members of the class survived into LMS days. Although withdrawals continued, one class member, by then numbered 5001, lasted until 1934 when it had to be renumbered 25001, as a new Stanier 'Black Five' 4-6-0 had been allocated 5001.

The famous 1892-built *Hardwicke*, which carried the LMS number 5031, was a late withdrawal in 1932 and was one of a very select number of historic engines that even the LMS did not feel ought to be scrapped.

It was put to one side at Crewe works but very rarely saw the light of day until it was eventually put on public display in the new Museum of British Transport at Clapham in 1962. However, on closure of Clapham in preparation for the opening of the National Railway Museum at York, *Hardwicke* was not moved to York but instead went to Steamtown at Carnforth on August 4, 1974, where it was returned to steam the following summer after

more than 40 years.

Essentially this was to enable it to take part in the Rail 150 Stockton & Darlington cavalcade at Shildon on August 31, 1975.

TEST RUN

It was fully main line certified and after a test run up the Cumbrian Coast on July 22 in pouring rain with a GER coach, *Hardwicke* set off for Shildon on August 17, 1975 piloting LNER A3 Pacific No. 4472 *Flying Scotsman*, this time with a Caledonian coach.

Following the cavalcade, *Hardwicke* took its place in the NRM but even greater things were to come, and it returned to Carnforth on April 24, 1976, this time piloting MR Compound 4-4-0 No. 1000 on a railtour from York. It had further outings on the Cumbrian Coast including solo shuttles from Carnforth to Grange-over-Sands and returned to York in June piloting BR Standard 9F 2-10-0 No. 92220 *Evening Star*.

No. 790 then led a quieter existence but was still steamed and worked occasionally on the Derwent Valley Light Railway at York. For its appearance in the 1980 Rocket 150 Liverpool & Manchester cavalcade at Rainhill, *Hardwicke* was matched with three LNWR Royal Train carriages. Unfortunately, what should have been a triumphant finale on the LNWR route across the Pennines with Stanier Pacific No. 46229 *Duchess of Hamilton*, had to be diesel hauled because of a fire risk.

Hardwicke spent the rest of 1980 at the Dinting Railway Centre but returned to York and retired to life as a static exhibit, more recently at the Locomotion museum in Shildon.

BELOW: In LMS livery, Webb Coal Tank No. 7799 departs from Keighley on the KWVR in October 2012.

Coal Tank 0-6-2T No. 1054

BETWEEN 1881 AND 1897, Crewe built 300 of Webb's Coal Tanks, a side tank version of his standard 17in coal engine 0-6-0, with the same cheaply produced cast-iron wheels and H-section spokes.

Eight were withdrawn by the LNWR before Grouping, but 64 were inherited by BR in 1948 and the last survivor, the 250th to be built, was withdrawn from Abergavenny shed in 1958.

This engine had entered service in 1888 as No. 1054 and worked in the Midlands and various parts of Wales before being withdrawn in 1939. However, wartime locomotive shortages saw it overhauled and reinstated in December 1940.

It became even more widely travelled, mostly on former LNWR routes, and found itself at Shrewsbury, working local passenger trains to Craven Arms, before moving to Abergavenny. After 12 months on loan to the NCB at Windsor Colliery near Pontypridd, it found itself alone at Abergavenny as the last survivor of the class, carrying the BR number 58926.

It famously worked the Stephenson Locomotive Society's last train on the Abergavenny to Merthyr line on January 5, 1958 with 'Super D' 0-8-0 No. 49121 and was withdrawn from Pontypool in 1958.

GENTLE AND HOMELY RELIC

There the story might have ended, but for a group of determined enthusiasts headed by Max Dunn, the former shedmaster at Bangor shed, who was persuaded to organise an appeal to raise funds to buy No. 58926. He was quoted in a letter: "The British Transport Commission require £666 for this engine in order to satisfy their auditors, and are pressing for a substantial remittance on account. Please send what you can afford to save this gentle and homely relic of a more tranquil age from the oxy-acetylene cutting apparatus."

The appeal was successful, and he arranged for it to go to Hednesford in Staffordshire for safe storage by the Railway Preservation Society from 1961 to 1963, which was later to become the Chasewater Light Railway.

The engine was transferred into the ownership of the National Trust, and repainted in LNWR livery as No. 1054 at Crewe, for display at Penrhyn Castle in North Wales, not far from where the engine worked in the 1920s.

With the growth of active railway preservation groups, some of the locomotive's original trustees arranged for it to be loaned to the Bahamas Locomotive Society at Dinting Railway Centre, where it arrived on September 22, 1973, and where a return to steam might be possible.

Its overhaul was completed in 1980, the engine restored to the LNWR condition in which it would have appeared just before the First World War. In May that year it took part in the Rocket 150 cavalcade at Rainhill commemorating the opening of the Liverpool and Manchester Railway in 1830.

No. 1054 worked one-coach trains on the main line in the summer

ABOVE: No. 1054 approaches Ingrow on the KWVR on June 21, 1986. Four years later Ingrow was to become the engine's permanent home.

ABOVE: No. 1054 pilots 0-8-0 No. 49395 away from Furnace Sidings on the Pontypool & Blaenavon Railway on September 14, 2013.

Ingrow on the KWVR in 1990. As well as working on the KWVR, the engine visited the Llangollen and Battlefield Line railways.

RETURNED TO ACTIVE SERVICE

No. 1054 needed a further overhaul after 1999 and with Heritage Lottery Fund assistance this was completed by the society at Ingrow and the engine returned to active service in February 2011. It has carried unlined LNWR black, BR black and LMS black liveries (as No. 7799), and was able to pilot the National Collection's LNWR 'Super D' 0-8-0 No. 49395 in a recreation of the 1958 railtour at the nearby Pontypool & Blaenavon Railway in September 2013.

'Super D' 0-8-0 No. 49395

THE HISTORY OF THE LNWR 0-8-0s is complicated but they were the workhorses of the railway's coal and heavy goods traffic for many years, continuing through LMS days, and right up to withdrawal of the last four from Bescot shed in 1964.

Webb built 282 0-8-0s, which were of two types, all except the first one were compounds. One hundred and eleven of them had two high-pressure cylinders outside the frames and one low-pressure cylinder inside, which were known as Class A from 1911, while there were 170 Class B engines with two inside low-pressure cylinders.

Webb's successor, George Whale, was appointed in April 1903 and is credited with the development of Webb's Precedent 2-4-0 into the Precursor 4-4-0 and the commencement of the conversion of the many varieties of LNWR heavy freight 0-8-0s into what eventually became known as the G2 class. He served until 1909 when Charles Bowen Cooke took over.

Bowen Cooke added superheating to Whale's Precursor to produce the George V 4-4-0 but his main claim to fame was the impressive, if not particularly effective, four-cylindered Claughton 4-6-0, introduced in 1913.

Hewitt Pearson Montague Beames then served only briefly as CME and when the LNWR merged with the Lancashire &

Yorkshire Railway in 1922, it was the L&Y man, George Hughes who took over and subsequently became the first CME of the LMS.

When George Whale took over, he began rebuilding the 0-8-0s in several ways. Thirty-six Class Bs became 2-8-0s but remained as Compounds but 10 of those converted from May 1906 were provided with larger boilers and were later designated Class F. Twenty-six retained their original boilers and were later designated Class E.

The Class As were rebuilt as four-cylindered simple 0-8-0s with their original

> *The LMS inherited 91 unsuperheated engines in 1923 but rebuilt them all to G1 between 1924 and 1937*

boilers, and designated Class C. However, 62 Class As were given larger boilers and became Class D. The last 34 conversions from Class A to simples with original boilers became Class C1 as their new cylinders were a different size.

The Class Bs were then rebuilt as 0-8-0 two-cylindered simples with the larger boiler

becoming Class G with 60 new Class Gs built in 1910. The first of the Class Gs was fitted with superheating and became G1 in 1912. The LMS inherited 91 unsuperheated engines in 1923 but rebuilt them all to G1 between 1924 and 1937.

HIGHER PRESSURE BOILERS

A further 170 G1s were built between 1912 and 1918 but the LNWR started building G2 0-8-0s in 1921-1922, with higher pressure boilers. It built 60 in total, which uniquely among the LNWR 0-8-0s, were never rebuilt from or into other classes. However, most of the G1s and G2s were fitted with Belpaire boilers by the LMS from 1936 and became G2As, but some of the G2As received low-pressure boilers on overhaul, and reverted to G1. BR inherited 320 G2As, the largest ex-LNWR class to run on BR, but the G1s and G2As used the same number series.

Although these are the official LNWR, LMS and BR classifications for the engines, in LNWR days, all the 0-8-0 classes tended to be called Class D whether they were or not and those that received superheating were all known as 'Super Ds', a name that has stuck, among other less-flattering nicknames.

In fact the last development of the LNWR 0-8-0, the Belpaire-boilered two-cylindered

BELOW: LNWR 'Super D' 0-8-0 No. 49395 passes Quorn & Woodhouse on the Great Central Railway with a goods train in February 2008.

ABOVE: LNWR 'Super D' 0-8-0 No. 49395 approaches Furnace Sidings on the Pontypool & Blaenavon Railway with a goods train in September 2013.

G2A is far removed from actually being a 'Super D' which was a four-cylinder rebuild of an original Webb Compound 0-8-0.

The first of the new G2 class, built by the LNWR as No. 485 in 1921 was selected for official preservation as the ultimate development of the 0-8-0 type by the LNWR, although the LMS developed the design further. Withdrawn from Buxton shed as No. 49395 in very poor condition, after sustaining a cracked cylinder in an accident on the Ashbourne-Buxton line in 1959, it was stored at Crewe works for a while, moving to Stratford in January 1965.

It became one of the most neglected engines in the National Collection despite quickly being selected for display in a new museum in Leicester. It moved to storage in the Midland roundhouse at Leicester in November 1967 but when the museum's plans had to be scaled down, the G2 returned to the National Collection store, by now at Preston Park, in September 1970. With the museum's plans resuscitated, No. 49395 moved back to Leicester in August 1972 but only for another four years in storage.

A more positive move to an engineering works locomotive shed at Horsehay near Telford on February 19, 1976, could have seen the engine restored to work on a heritage line being planned in the area but it was not to be. It made a short journey to the Telford Industrial Museum at Blists Hill on September 14, 1981 where it was at least on public display, although still not restored.

VIRTUALLY BEYOND REDEMPTION
The increasingly derelict hulk then moved to Tyseley in 1988 and then on to the Midland

> *The first of the new class built by the LNWR as No. 485 in 1921 was selected for official preservation as the ultimate development of the 0-8-0 type by the LNWR...*

Railway Centre at Butterley on July 4, 1990 but it was considered virtually beyond redemption. However, in 1993, Pete Waterman, who remembered the class with affection from his trainspotting days, offered to pay for the overhaul; new welding techniques now facilitating an effective repair to the damaged cylinder. The engine was moved to the NRM at York in March and work finally started.

The cylinder was successfully repaired, but it was never plain sailing, the restoration stalled and the deal between the museum and Waterman was renegotiated in 1997 with Pete's LNWR works at Crewe taking over some of the work. The chassis was delivered in May 2002 for reassembly, and the complete engine was unveiled at Crewe on June 8, 2005. It entered traffic on the nearby Churnet Valley Railway on July 14.

It has since spent periods in regular use on the North Yorkshire Moors and East Lancashire railways as well as visiting many other lines, but is now in need of a further overhaul, terms for which have yet to be agreed. In the meantime it is on display at the Locomotion museum at Shildon.

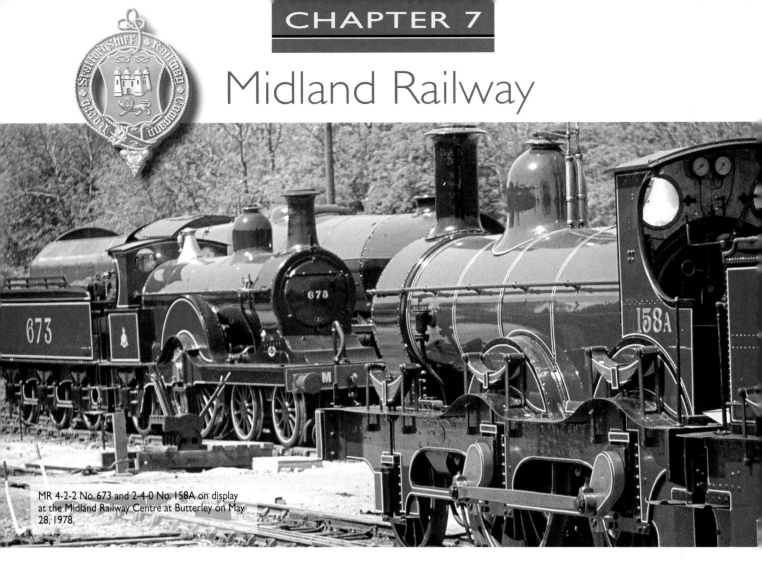

MR 4-2-2 No. 673 and 2-4-0 No. 158A on display at the Midland Railway Centre at Butterley on May 28, 1978.

THE MIDLAND RAILWAY came into being in 1844 as a result of the merger of the Midland Counties Railway, the North Midland Railway, and the Birmingham and Derby Junction Railway. These met at Derby, where the MR established its headquarters and locomotive works. Its main line initially ran from London to Leeds via the East Midlands along what is now the Midland Main Line. It ended up with a large network of lines radiating from the East Midlands to connect with Birmingham, Bristol, York, Manchester and eventually Carlisle.

It became the third-largest railway company in the British Isles (after the Great Western and the LNWR), the largest coal haulier and the largest British railway to have its headquarters outside London.

Involved from the start was 'Railway King' George Hudson from the North Midland, who was later to die in disgrace in Paris after serving time in York prison. In its earliest days the MR controlled all the traffic from London to the North East and Scotland, but the LNWR was progressing slowly through the Lake District with what would become the WCML, and there was pressure for a direct line from London to York and this would become the ECML.

After Hudson's departure in disgrace, having sabotaged the company for his own ends and assisting in the building of competing routes, the MR struggled but survived largely thanks to the financial acumen of John Ellis from the Midland Counties Railway. It had the advantage over the competition in terms of the lucrative coal traffic to London and this took precedence over passenger traffic, which was hit hard by the opening of the Great Northern route from King's Cross to Yorkshire, the MR still relying on the LNWR for its access to London itself via Rugby.

The LNWR, MR, GNR and MSLR fought bitterly and alliances between two or more companies against the others were made and broken, resulting in episodes such as the Euston Square Confederacy (LNWR, MR and MSLR against GNR) and later the Cheshire Lines Committee (MR, GNR & MSLR against LNWR).

The MR wanted its own route to London and started with the Leicester and Hitchin Railway from Wigston to Market Harborough and Bedford, joining the GN at Hitchin for King's Cross. Through MR services to London were introduced in 1858. It had to be followed by a new line from Bedford, to a new terminus at St Pancras, completed in 1868, right alongside King's Cross but a far more impressive terminus.

The MR reached Manchester from Derby via Peak Forest in 1866 and Sheffield finally got its station in 1870. In the 1870s another dispute with the LNWR led the MR to construct the Settle and Carlisle line, to secure its access to Scotland, creating the highest main line in England.

The MR was a successful and profitable railway but became too busy for its own good. It introduced a centralised traffic control system, and the locomotive power classifications that were used up to the end of BR steam. It pioneered gas lighting on trains, put third-class carriages on all its trains in 1872 and abolished second class in 1875. It led the way in the use of bogie coaches and introduced Pullman cars.

The Midland Railway always used the term 'engine', not locomotive and was noted for its small-engine policy, briefly adopted by the LMS, to the regret of staff from the LNWR.

In 1907 MR locomotives were renumbered in a systematic way, each class in a consecutive sequence, classes being ordered by type (passenger/tank/goods), power and age. After the Grouping this system was adapted for the whole of the LMS and later BR. The MR was unique in that its engines carried a cast numberplate on the smokebox door as opposed to a painted number on the bufferbeam. They also carried a cast shedplate and both these features were adopted by the LMS, again uniquely among the Big Four companies but used as standard across the whole of the BR system after 1948.

The MR originally painted its engines green but this changed to crimson lake by 1883. This colour was chosen by the LMS for its passenger locomotives and coaches, and after Nationalisation, coaches from 1957 on most regions used LMS maroon, derived from the Midland's colour.

The MR has fared well in preservation, its locomotives, their livery, its architectural style, its signalboxes and signals were all some of the most distinctive in Britain, and this is reflected in the heritage lines that have opened on Midland routes; notably the Keighley & Worth Valley Railway and nearby Embsay & Bolton Abbey Steam Railway.

The Midland Railway Centre, now Midland Railway-Butterley was conceived as a showcase for MR heritage while Peak Rail runs on part of the MR main line to Manchester. The Ecclesbourne Valley, Avon Valley Railway and Rushden Railway Museum run on MR routes. The Battlefield line was joint MR/LNWR and a Midland roundhouse was a latecomer to the heritage portfolio in the shape of the Barrow Hill Roundhouse.

2-4-0 No. 158A

MATTHEW KIRTLEY had impeccable railway credentials, having started work on the Stockton and Darlington Railway at the age of 13. He was a fireman on the Liverpool and Manchester Railway, attended its opening, and eventually became a driver on the London and Birmingham Railway, where he is believed to have driven the first L&BR train (in fact the first main line train) to enter London.

He became the MR's locomotive superintendent and his locomotive designs were to survive well into LMS days. Kirtley's brother and nephew were also noted locomotive engineers.

Twenty-nine of Kirtley's 156 class 2-4-0s were built at Derby between 1866 and 1874 for express passenger duties which, until 1868, involved working to King's Cross. Of these 21 survived into LMS days, by then only performing menial duties. However, the LMS recognised the significance of the class and pioneer No. 156 was earmarked for preservation but this decision was overturned and the engine was scrapped in 1932. However, 15 years later longlived surviving classmate No. 20002 finally ended its days at Nottingham as station pilot after 81 years' service and was set aside at Derby.

Despite having been reboilered twice, its front-end being much rebuilt, and having a new tender, it was restored to MR condition as No. 158A and put into store.

March 17, 1965 saw it transferred to the National Collection store in the old MR shed at Hellifield but it quickly moved to the MR roundhouse at Leicester on August 22, 1967 and was put on display

ABOVE: 2-4-0 No. 158A on display at Swanwick Junction at the Midland Railway-Butterley in April 2015.

in a small museum in the city on February 28, 1968. Closure of this museum saw the engine move to the Midland Railway Centre at Butterley in 1975 where it remained on display. It is now considered too fragile to move, other than occasionally being positioned outside for vintage train events.

1377 class 0-6-0T No. 41708

AFTER holding senior positions on several other railways, in 1873 Samuel Johnson became locomotive superintendent of the MR, where he would stay until his retirement in 1904.

Johnson introduced the 1377 class 0-6-0T in 1878 based on an 1874 design. By 1891 185 had been built, mostly at Derby, but the last 20 by Vulcan Foundry. Most were built without a rear to the cab becoming known as 'half-cabs'. Most were built with round-topped fireboxes, but many later with Belpaire fireboxes. Although withdrawals started in 1928, no fewer than 87 of the 1F 0-6-0Ts were inherited by BR but by 1961 only 11 remained in service.

However, they became one of the oldest classes in BR service as five remained in use until 1966. A contract had been signed by the MR in 1866 to provide shunting engines to Staveley Ironworks for 100 years and this was honoured by BR.

On withdrawal of these five in December 1966 one, which had originally been No. 1418, but renumbered 1708 in 1907, and allocated to Barrow Hill throughout its BR days, was purchased for preservation and by June 1967 had arrived on the KWVR where it was returned to steam in February 1969. It was to have a very active retirement.

Rather small for KWVR services, it moved to Derby works on December 14, 1974 where it joined the collection of engines being assembled for the Midland Railway project, which was by then focusing its attention on the branch through Butterley.

However, it was moved instead to Dunstable in March 1976 where it was housed on a cement works siding, but eventually moved to Butterley in March 1979, though it was not steamed there until November 1984. It was hired to the Swanage Railway, which was in its infancy at the time, but short of motive power and able to use locomotives of limited

LEFT: MR 1F 0-6-0T No. 41708 at Workington steelworks in September 2002.

power on its then short length of line. A further move to the Dean Forest Railway on March 22, 1995 saw the engine move a bit nearer to MR territory as similar engines once shunted the MR's Gloucester docks branch, but it returned to Swanage on February 23, 1997 for further service as well as paying a visit to Llangollen and later the North Norfolk Railway.

Finally the engine returned home to the newly opened Barrow Hill Roundhouse at Staveley, opposite the site of its former home turf at the ironworks where it was a popular choice as shed pilot at occasional open days and photo charters. Since its boiler certificate expired the engine has remained on static exhibition and there are still no firm plans for an overhaul.

ABOVE: MR 1F 0-6-0T No. 41708 heads a photo charter goods train at Parkend on the Dean Forest Railway in July 1995.

115 class 4-2-2 No. 673

FIFTEEN of Johnson's 115 class 4-2-2s were built in the three years from 1896 and could pull expresses of 200 to 250 tons at up to 90mph and their huge single driving wheels at speed led to them being nicknamed 'Spinners'. They worked for up to 30 years into LMS days, usually as pilot engines in later years as trains got heavier; some even as pilots on coal trains.

Twelve of the class survived the Grouping, but by 1927 only three remained, and when the last one, No. 673 was withdrawn in 1928, it was set aside at Derby for preservation, and restored to MR livery with its original number 118.

March 17, 1965 saw it transferred to the National Collection store in the old MR shed at Hellifield along with Kirtley's 2-4-0 No. 158A but it quickly moved to the MR shed at Leicester on August 22, 1967 and was put on display in a small museum in the city on February 28, 1968.

Closure of this museum saw the engine move to the Midland Railway Centre at Butterley in 1975 where it remained on display. May 1978, however, saw it returned to steam as No. 673 although sadly it never pulled a public passenger train.

It travelled to Rainhill for the L&MR Rocket 150 cavalcade in May 1980, in the company of LMS 4F 0-6-0 No. 4027 and SDJR 7F 2-8-0 No. 13809. Although diesel-hauled this was only because of fire risk and in fact the diesel pilot was commandeered for another job allowing the trebleheader led by No. 673 to work for a short distance unassisted from Chinley.

No. 673 had one more main line run, from Butterley to Tinsley open day in June 1980 along with the 4F but then moved to the NRM at York under its own steam in October 1980 where it was put on display and has not been steamed since.

Johnson was to have considerable influence on later MR locomotive design, which was to continue well into LMS days. He designed the 483 class 4-4-0 for passenger work and this formed the basis for the later LMS 2P 4-4-0; the 2441 class 0-6-0T in 1899, originally with round-topped fireboxes, but rebuilt by Fowler with Belpaire fireboxes, on which Fowler's 'Jinty' 3F was based, and the 3835 class 0-6-0 for freight work in 1911, which continued to be built up to 1941 by the LMS as the Fowler 4F.

ABOVE: MR 4-2-2 No. 673 in steam at the Midland Railway Centre at Butterley on May 28, 1978.

ABOVE: MR 4F 0-6-0 No. 43924 crosses Mytholmes viaduct on the Keighley and Worth Valley Railway in December 2014.

3835 class 0-6-0 No. 43924

HENRY FOWLER, born in Evesham in 1870, served an apprenticeship under John Aspinall at the Lancashire and Yorkshire Railway's Horwich works from 1887 to 1891, and succeeded George Hughes as head of the testing department after four years. On June 18, 1900 he joined the MR and rose by 1909 to succeed Richard Deeley as CME.

Between 1915 and 1919 Fowler was employed on war work and James Anderson became acting CME. In 1919, Fowler was made a KBE for his contributions to the war effort, and his influence on MR locomotive design was to last well into LMS days.

The 3835 class 0-6-0 was to become one of Britain's best-known steam designs, lasting until well after its sell-by date on freight work. Fowler built the first two in 1911 but the class eventually totalled 197 engines, five built by Armstrong Whitworth for the Somerset and Dorset Joint Railway. The MR ones were numbered 3835-4026.

After Fowler's appointment as CME of the LMS in 1925, he continued to build basically similar engines for LMS service. The MR-built ones were withdrawn by 1965 but one, No. 43924, built in 1920, found its way to Barry scrapyard and was famously the first engine to be purchased from the yard for preservation, by the 4F Society, arriving on the KWVR on September 11, 1968, just a month after the end of BR steam.

Not having had so long to deteriorate as later purchases from the yard, and with spare parts rather more readily available, the unique Midland 4F was back in steam by June 1974 as No. 3924 and has been in regular service on the line for much of the past 45 years. The engine was finally purchased by the KWVR from the original owners in 1990.

Being the ideal size, appropriate to the line and of simple design and construction, whenever it becomes due for overhaul it tends to be the favourite choice and rarely remains in the queue or in Haworth works for too long. The last overhaul was completed in 2011 and in BR livery, No. 43924 is currently hard at work, making its first-ever visit to another heritage line in September 2014 for the Severn Valley steam gala.

ABOVE: No. 43924 crosses Mytholmes viaduct with a goods train at the KWVR steam gala 38 years earlier on April 4, 1976.

ABOVE: No. 43924 climbs away from Keighley on the KWVR.

ABOVE: No. 1000 and LMS Jubilee 4-6-0 No. 5690 *Leander* tackle Ulverston bank on the Cumbrian Coast line on May 5, 1980.

Compound 4-4-0 No. 1000

IN 1875 RICHARD Deeley became a pupil of Samuel Johnson at Derby works, eventually replacing Johnson as locomotive superintendent on January 1, 1904. He continued and developed the company's use of compound 4-4-0s started by Johnson but disagreed with the MR board over its small-engine policy and resigned at the end of 1909.

Five 4-4-0s were built in 1902 by Samuel Johnson with a three-cylinder compound arrangement and one high-pressure cylinder inside the frames, and two low-pressure cylinders outside, utilising Smith's starting arrangement. Johnson's successor, Deeley, built an enlarged and simplified version, using his own starting arrangement, making the engines simpler to drive. These locomotives were originally numbered 1000-1029, but in 1907 during a renumbering scheme the five Smith/Johnson locomotives became 1000-1004 and the Deeley compounds 1005-1034, 10 more of these being added in 1908-09. They retained their MR numbers under the LMS, which continued to build slightly modified Compounds; although these were of MR design, they were extensively used on WCML services.

The original Johnson locomotives were all subsequently rebuilt as Deeley compounds, including the now-preserved No. 1000 which was rebuilt with a superheater in 1914.

The original MR engines retained the numbers 1000-1044 into LMS days, but the LMS-built ones would become BR Nos. 40900-39 and 41045-41199. The original ones were all withdrawn by early BR days, and the very first, despite having been significantly rebuilt,

It even became one of a very select number of BR's preserved engines to be returned to steam.

was withdrawn in 1951 but retained at Derby for preservation, eventually being restored to MR livery in 1914 condition as No. 1000. It even became one of a very select number of BR's preserved engines to be returned to steam, working occasional railtours from 1959 until put on static display in the Museum of British Transport at Clapham in 1962.

On closure of the museum, No. 1000 was moved by rail to the new NRM at York on April 19, 1975 and returned to steam for

the Rail 150 S&D cavalcade at Shildon in August 1975. From April 1976 it was used in occasional railtour service once again, but always doubleheaded, although it made a couple of solo runs on private charter trains. It was loaned to the Dinting Railway Centre from October 1978 to May 1979, working both ways from York on tours with LMS Jubilee 4-6-0 No. 5690 *Leander* and appeared in the Rocket 150 cavalcade at Rainhill in May 1980.

Its finale was a pair of runs over the Settle & Carlisle line in February 1982 in snowy conditions also accompanied by *Leander*. It proved the efficiency of the compound design by using only 1500 gallons of water on this run over this arduous route.

Since then, No. 1000 has been on display at the NRM, Bo'ness, the SVR Engine House and at Barrow Hill, but it has never worked on a preserved line.

Compound locomotives

MOST STEAM locomotives are 'simple', i.e. the steam drives the piston in the cylinder and is immediately exhausted. In a compound steam engine, steam is expanded in two or more stages. Typically, the steam is first expanded in a high-pressure cylinder, then having given up heat and pressure, it exhausts directly into one or more larger low-pressure cylinders, before being exhausted. Such engines are complicated but far more economical to operate.

Compounding was first used in stationary

engines, and was popular in marine applications, but while its use in railway engines was widespread in France and the US, it never caught on widely on Britain's railways, and the only longlived British class of compounds were the MR 4-4-0s.

A compound locomotive has separate valve gear for its high- and low-pressure cylinders and in some cases these can be operated independently by the driver, which can be of assistance in getting a train on the move.

LEFT: MR Compound 4-4-0 No. 1000 and LNER V2 2-6-2 No. 4771 *Green Arrow* speed through Calverley cutting north of Leeds on May 3, 1980.

LEFT: On a rare solo outing, No. 1000 departs from Harrogate with a private charter on October 7, 1981.

LEFT: On its final railtour working, No. 1000 and No. 5690 *Leander* top Ais Gill summit with a 'Cumbrian Mountain Express' on February 12, 1983.

CHAPTER 8

Lancashire & Yorkshire Railway

ABOVE: In BR livery, L&Y 0-6-0 No. 52044 crosses Mytholmes viaduct on the KWVR with a goods train. GEOFF LEE

THE LANCASHIRE and Yorkshire Railway was incorporated from an amalgamation of several existing railways in 1847, particularly the Manchester and Leeds Railway, to become the third-largest railway system in northern England after the MR and North Eastern Railway.

Its system, as the name suggests, served the major conurbations of Merseyside, Lancashire and West Yorkshire and consisted of the most complex and densely trafficked network of routes in Britain. For this it owned 1650 locomotives, more per mile than any other company. Its number of passenger services was exceeded only by the LNWR, MR and GWR. It was the first main line railway to electrify some of its lines, and was a bigger shipowner than any other British railway company.

It had only one route across the Pennines between Lancashire and Yorkshire, through the 2885-yard Summit Tunnel and its Manchester

Victoria station was one of the largest in the country at the time, with 17 platforms. The L&Y carriage and wagon works at Newton Heath had a football team that would eventually evolve into Manchester United.

The L&Y's locomotive works were originally at Miles Platting, but were moved to Horwich in 1889. Its locomotives were originally dark green with ornate brasswork with black and white lining, then light green, but from 1883 all locomotives were painted black, with red and white lining for passenger engines and red lining only or plain black for goods engines.

The L&Y amalgamated with the LNWR on January 1, 1922, just before the Grouping, and the LNWR's chief mechanical engineer and other senior positions were created from the L&Y during that year. Its basic system has survived remarkably well despite branch closures resulting from the rundown of traditional heavy industries, especially coal. Today the one-time L&Y East Lancashire Railway based at Bury, despite being a late starter, has become the premier LMS heritage line.

Class 25 0-6-0 No. 957

WILLIAM BARTON Wright was locomotive superintendent of the L&Y from 1876 to 1886. He introduced the Class 25 0-6-0 in 1876 and 280 were built, mostly by outside contractors, acquiring the nickname 'Ironclads'. No fewer than 230 were later converted to saddle tanks by John Aspinall, to become Class 23, after he had designed an improved 0-6-0. Withdrawals started in 1930 but 23 of the original 0-6-0s survived into BR ownership in 1948.

The last survivor, Wakefield-based Beyer Peacock-built No. 52044 was bought for preservation in 1959 by Tony Cox, a founder member of the Lancashire & Yorkshire Railway Preservation Society and, after a period of being stored at Horwich, moved to Ranskill near Retford in 1961, then to the NCB's Walton colliery near Wakefield before arriving on the KWVR on January 7, 1965 when locomotives and stock were being assembled before reopening the line.

It was soon put in steam in June 1965 and worked not only occasional members' trains but famously starred alongside Jenny Agutter in the film classic The Railway Children in 1970 as the 'Green Dragon' in green livery.

It made a brief return to service in BR

ABOVE: L&Y 0-6-0 No. 957 heads a train of three L&Y coaches away from Oakworth on the Keighley and Worth Valley Railway.

livery in 1975 but went to the SVR for overhaul in December 1996 after acquisition by the Bowers Trust, where two of the three trustees were provided by the KWVR and the Lancashire & Yorkshire Railway Trust. The work was completed at Bridgnorth and the

engine returned to service on the KWVR in April 2002 again in BR livery.

A repaint to fully lined-out L&Y passenger colours as No. 957 followed but its boiler certificate expired in early 2013 and it is now awaiting overhaul.

BELOW: L&Y 0-6-0 No. 957 departs from Keighley with a KWVR vintage train.

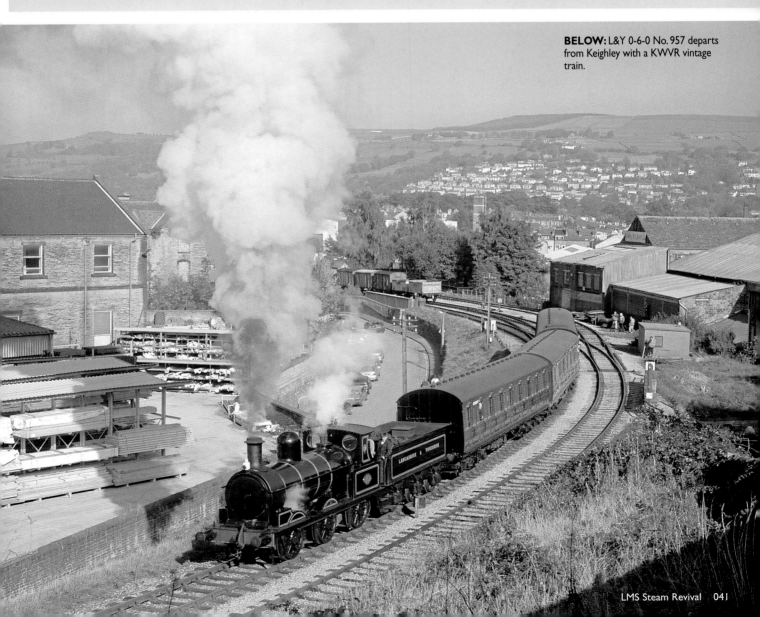

LEFT: L&Y 0-6-0ST No. 752 in steam at Haworth on the KWVR on March 27, 1982.

JOHN AUDLEY FREDERICK Aspinall, born in 1851 was apprenticed to John Ramsbottom and Francis Webb of the LNWR in 1868 and served as locomotive superintendent of the Great Southern and Western Railway in Ireland. He is noted for having introduced vacuum brakes to his locomotives in Ireland, which were to become standard on most railways in Britain.

He became the L&Y's chief mechanical engineer in 1886 and its general manager in 1899. Aspinall received a knighthood in 1917 for his contributions to the war effort and national transport system.

Class 23 0-6-0ST No. 752

THE CLASS 23 0-6-0STs for shunting and short-trip freight working were rebuilds by Aspinall between 1891 and 1900, using the frames and wheels from earlier Barton Wright 0-6-0 tender engines. The 0-6-0STs proved longlived, and although the first withdrawal was by the LMS in 1926, 101 survived until Nationalisation with the last withdrawn by BR in 1964.

No. 752 was built in 1881 by Beyer Peacock as one of the Class 25 0-6-0 tender engines like No. 957 but was rebuilt in April 1896 as a saddle tank. It was withdrawn by the LMS from the Wigan area as No. 11456 in 1937 but was sold to The Blainscough Colliery Company for its Welch Whittle Colliery near Wigan.

It later worked for the NCB at Chisnall Hall and Standish collieries, Parsonage Colliery and and a brief spell at Bickershaw Colliery, but it was out of use by 1958, though not scrapped, and was still in existence in 1966.

The L&Y Saddletanks Fund negotiated with the NCB for more than two years before the NCB was convinced of the preservationists' serious intention to restore it but then generously agreed to donate it.

The engine was moved by rail, by a very devious route through Lancashire in April 1968, part of the journey with haulage by LMS 8F 2-8-0 No. 48773, to Yates Duxbury's paper mills at Heap Bridge near Heywood, where restoration started. It was moved by road to the KWVR in 1971 for completion of its overhaul and was returned to steam in 1977 and able to participate in the Rocket 150 cavalcade at Rainhill in 1980, after which it saw limited service on the KWVR for a couple of years.

Extensive boiler repairs were necessary and so the fund became the L&YRPS and an L&YR Trust was formed, which became a registered charity and made a successful application to the Heritage Lottery Fund. The boiler work was carried out by Alan McEwan while other work was undertaken on the ELR and at the KWVR, and a return to steam is imminent.

Class 5 2-4-2T No. 1008

ASPINALL DESIGNED the Class 5 2-4-2T and 270 were built from 1889 onwards, with various modifications, some being fitted for push-pull working. In 1905, Hughes built another 40 with Belpaire rather than round-topped fireboxes and from 1910, this boiler was also fitted to rebuilt locomotives. One hundred and ten eventually came into BR ownership in 1948 and three lasted until 1961.

However, the first of the class, which had become BR No. 50621, happened to be the first locomotive to be constructed at Horwich works and on withdrawal in 1954, it was retained at the works and restored to L&Y livery as No. 1008. It joined other National Collection locomotives at Stratford works in October 1964, moving on to Preston Park on February 19, 1968, before being placed on

ABOVE: LYR 2-4-2T No. 1008 on display in the National Railway Museum at York.

loan to the Birmingham Railway Museum at Tyseley on September 7, 1970 where it was displayed at occasional open days.

No. 1008 moved to the NRM at York in 1976 where it remains on display but it has never been steamed in preservation.

18in gauge 0-4-0ST *Wren*

HORWICH works had an extensive 18in-gauge internal railway system and Aspinall ordered steam engines to work this system. The first two, *Robin* and *Wren* came from Beyer Peacock in 1886, followed by *Dot*, and five more were built at Horwich.

Among their duties was the distribution of wage packets around the works. Withdrawn in 1962, *Wren* is on display in the National Railway Museum at York.

LEFT: Narrow gauge L&Y 0-4-0ST *Wren* in the entrance hall of the NRM.

ABOVE: L&Y Class 27 0-6-0 No. 1300 pilots 4F No. 43924 away from Keighley on the KWVR.

ABOVE: L&Y 0-4-0ST No. 51218 on the Bristol Harbour Railway.

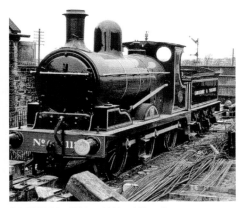

ABOVE: No. 1300 as 1122 at White Bear.
BILL ASHCROFT

RIGHT: BR livery, L&Y 0-6-0 No. 52322 heads a photo charter goods train into Nuttall Tunnel on the East Lancashire Railway in October 1995.

Class 21 0-4-0ST

FIFTY-SEVEN of Aspinall's Class 21 0-4-0STs were built at Horwich between 1891 and 1910, designed for shunting in tightly curved sidings in docks and goods yards. They acquired the nickname 'Pugs'. Used by the L&Y at Fleetwood, Goole, Liverpool and Salford, they became much more widely dispersed in LMS days, reaching places such as Bristol, Bangor, Crewe, Derby, Widnes, York and Swansea. At Nationalisation 23 remained in service and the last was withdrawn by BR in 1964.

No. 11243

THE LANCASHIRE and Yorkshire Railway Trust also purchased L&Y No. 19 for preservation. This engine was built in 1910, but as No. 11243, was sold by the LMS in 1931 and was acquired by the trust from the United Glass Bottle Manufacturers at Charlton, London in 1967, moving via Luton to the KWVR. In poor condition it has not been returned to steam and has remained on static display, spending some time at the Steamport museum at Southport but more recently the Ribble Steam Railway.

Class 27 0-6-0 No. 52322

ASPINALL'S Class 27 0-6-0s totalling 484 engines, were built between 1889 and 1918 at Horwich, and became the L&Y's standard goods engine, with two cylinders, a non-superheated round-topped boiler and Joy's valve gear. After Aspinall became general manager of the L&Y on July 1, 1899, more were built under his successors, Henry Hoy and George Hughes, with some modifications; some being superheated and some having Belpaire fireboxes. Three hundred survived into LMS days and even in 1960, 50 were still running on BR.

No. 52322 was bought for preservation, one of the first of such private purchases and after storage at Horwich works, moved to Fairclough's civil engineering depot at the former L&Y White Bear station near Adlington in August 1960, where it carried the incorrect number 1122 in L&Y livery.

It was moved to Steamtown Carnforth in 1976, where it was returned to steam in April 1982, in L&Y livery with its correct number 1300. It saw little use at Carnforth and moved to the East Lancashire Railway in September 1995 where it ran in both BR condition as No. 52322 and as L&Y No. 1300.

Owned by Andy Booth since 2003, the engine has been based at both the Ribble Steam Railway and Embsay & Bolton Abbey Railway, running in BR livery, L&Y livery or as LMS No. 12322. It has also been seen on the Ecclesbourne Valley and Keighley & Worth Valley railways.

ABOVE: L&Y 0-4-0ST No. 18 on display at the Ribble Steam Railway at Preston.

Class 21 0-4-0ST No. 51218

BUILT BY the L&Y at Horwich as No. 68 in 1901, this engine became No. 11218 at the Grouping and was withdrawn by BR as No. 51218 from Neath, South Wales in 1964.

Purchased for preservation by the Lancashire & Yorkshire Railway Trust, No. 51218 was the first locomotive to arrive at the KWVR in January 1965. It was soon restored to working order but spent the 1967-69 period away from Haworth for two periods, on hire to Brown & Polsons in Trafford Park while its own

locomotives were unavailable and even hauling enthusiasts' brakevan specials on the Rochdale- Whitworth branch.

No. 51218 took part in the Rail 150 cavalcade at Shildon in August 1975, but the mid-1990s saw the first major overhaul since 963 taking place at Haworth and the ELR, returning to steam in late 1997, for a further period of service. The locomotive has carried its original identity of L&Y No. 68 since 2004, and requires a 10-year overhaul, which will commence once 0-6-0ST No. 752 is complete.

ABOVE: L&Y 0-4-0ST No. 51218 works a one-coach passenger train up the 1-in-58 out of Keighley on February 8, 2003. FRED KERR

CHAPTER 9

Somerset & Dorset Joint Railway

CREATED in 1862 the Somerset & Dorset Railway was an amalgamation between the Somerset Central Railwayw and the Dorset Central Railway. The former, originally a broad gauge line, linked Glastonbury with the Bristol & Exeter main line and Bristol Channel ports, while the Dorset Central Railway opened on November 1, 1860 from the LSWR at Wimborne, to Blandford Forum.

Both railways saw benefits in linking up so the SCR built a mixed-gauge line east to Cole on February 3, 1862, while the DCR opened a line from Templecombe to Cole on the same day. The LSWR worked the DCR's original line but the SCR worked the new part as well as its own line, and within six months they amalgamated as the Somerset & Dorset Railway. The new company opened from Blandford to Templecombe on August 31, 1863, linking the English and Bristol channels.

But the railway was not a financial success and building an extension from Evercreech Junction to Bath, opened on July 20, 1874, thus creating a through route from the Midlands to the South Coast, did not solve its problems. It went into receivership and in August 1875 was acquired jointly by the MR and the LSWR and renamed the Somerset and Dorset Joint Railway. The MR took charge of motive power, and the LSWR provided the infrastructure and rolling stock. It remained jointly owned by the LMS and the Southern Railway after the 1923 Grouping.

A steeply graded and scenic line, carrying heavy holiday traffic on summer Saturdays, with a remarkable variety of

The railway was not a success... and building an extension from Evercreech Junction to Bath... did not solve its problems

doubleheaders, it was always popular with enthusiasts, but as early as 1951, sections of the system started to close, and through services were diverted to other routes, including the famous Manchester-Bournemouth 'Pines Express' in 1962.

Despite a campaign against closure, and after a false start in the January, the whole of the S&D closed on March 7, 1966, apart from three very short sections that didn't not survive for long.

Preservation schemes have come and gone over the years; a site at Radstock in the 1970s was shortlived, however, trains do run over a short distance at Midsomer Norton South with plans to extend to Chilcompton. The North Dorset Railway has plans for a restored section of the S&D with Shillingstone as its headquarters, while the narrow gauge Gartell Light Railway runs on S&D trackbed near Templecombe.

ABOVE: The two surviving SDJR 7F 2-8-0s, Nos. 88 and 53809 at Minehead on the West Somerset. Railway. ALAN GRIEVE

7F 2-8-0

THE LONDON AND SOUTH Western Railway, was responsible for providing motive power for the line, but being particularly heavily graded, required something more substantial than the MR's typical small engines.

James Clayton, draughtsman at Derby, produced something very different to the standard Derby-designed engines of MR days, using a 2-8-0 wheel arrangement, the boiler from a compound 4-4-0 and Walschaerts valve gear. It still had the troublesome and small Derby axleboxes though.

The first six were built at Derby and numbered 80-85, but a later batch were ordered by the LMS from Robert Stephenson and Co in Darlington and built with larger boilers, although these too received small boilers between the 1930s and 1950s. The 1914-built batch was right-hand drive, while the 1925-built ones were left-hand drive.

They were successful working over the Mendip hills, but when tried on MR coal trains they were unsuitable, encouraging the MR to stick with its small engines. The LMS numbered them 9670-9680, but they were renumbered 13800-13810 in 1932, becoming 53800-53810 after Nationalisation.

The earlier engines were withdrawn first but the later ones lasted until 1963-64 just before closure of the S&D route, having become synonymous with this popular route with enthusiasts, and seeing increased use on passenger trains, particularly on summer Saturdays in BR days.

ABOVE: Somerset & Dorset 7F 2-8-0 No. 53808 under restoration at Washford on the West Somerset Railway on June 12, 1983.

No. 88

FORTUNATELY two of the last 7Fs to be withdrawn by BR found their way to Barry scrapyard and in 1968, the members of the Somerset & Dorset Railway Circle (now the Trust) decided to preserve one. The bid was successful and the chosen engine, No. 53808 was moved by rail from Barry in October 1970. It even moved to Bristol for an open day at Bath Road shed soon afterwards.

In 1975 though, the trust's lease of Radstock shed was terminated, and restoration work ceased for a time. The engine had to be moved again by rail, from Radstock via Frome and Taunton to the West Somerset Railway on January 8, 1976. A new base was set up by the trust at Washford on the WSR, which at the time was in its very early stages of preservation but would later become Britain's longest standard gauge heritage line.

The engine returned to steam in August 1987 and has seen regular service on the line since then. Initially turned out in BR black livery, No. 88 returned to service after an overhaul in December 2005 painted in S&DJR Prussian blue livery, which it never carried in service, as black had been adopted by the S&D as standard for goods engines before the introduction of the 7Fs.

No. 88 has made regular visits to other heritage lines but has been withdrawn for an overhaul, which is expected to be completed in time for the 50th anniversary of the closure of the S&D in 2016.

LEFT: Somerset & Dorset Prussian blue-liveried 7F 2-8-0 No. 88 departs from Minehead on the West Somerset Railway.

RIGHT: SDJR 7F 2-8-0 No. 53808 running as No. 53807 heads a goods train at Blue Anchor on the West Somerset Railway on September 7 1989.

ABOVE: No. 53809 on April 24, 1976 shortly after arrival at Kirk Smeaton for restoration.

LEFT: Somerset & Dorset 7F 2-8-0 No. 13809 approaches Hope station in Derbyshire on October 31, 1981.

No. 53809

NO. 89 WAS also one of the second batch built in 1925 with larger boilers by Robert Stephenson & Co at Darlington, and after a working life spent entirely on the S&D, was withdrawn in June 1964 and went with No. 53808 to Barry.

This second 7F at the scrapyard was overlooked by preservationists for many years surprisingly, but in 1975, No. 53809 was purchased by the late Frank Beaumont and moved to the former Hull & Barnsley Railway station at Kirk Smeaton in West Yorkshire in December that year, where restoration proceeded quickly.

It moved to the Midland Railway Centre on March 8, 1980 for the finishing touches, just in time to participate in the Rocket 150 cavalcade at

A change was made to BR livery while the engine was main line certified, but its main line career was relatively shortlived.

Rainhill. The locomotive had gained a main line certificate and made its main line railtour debut on May 2, 1981 running through the Hope Valley and on to York, the appearance of such an engine on the East Coast Main Line being perhaps one of the biggest surprises in preservation history.

A problem was found on one tour when the chimney proved too tall for a bridge at Miles Platting near Manchester and the top was sheared off. The tour continued to Carnforth though. Initially turned out in LMS livery as No. 13809, a change was made to BR livery while the engine was main line certified, but its main line career was relatively shortlived.

Now in the care of the 13809 Locomotive Group, based at Butterley, a further overhaul was completed in January 2006, and it emerged again in BR black livery, spending a couple of seasons working on the North Yorkshire Moors Railway. A third overhaul is expected to be completed at Butterley in early 2016.

ABOVE: Somerset & Dorset 7F 2-8-0 No. 53809 on display at Bath Green Park station in March 2006.

LEFT: No. 53809 approaches Foley Park tunnel on the SVR on October 25, 1987.

ABOVE: Somerset & Dorset 7F 2-8-0 No. 53809 heads past Kettlesbeck Bridge near Clapham on the Carnforth-Hellifield line on August 16, 1986.

ABOVE: Somerset & Dorset 7F 2-8-0 No. 53809 pilots SR Bulleid Merchant Navy Pacific No. 35005 *Canadian Pacific* out of Nuttall Tunnel on the East Lancashire Railway on August 13, 1993.

Furness Railway

THE FURNESS RAILWAY originated as a mineral line from Kirkby-in-Furness to Dalton-in-Furness. It was extended from Dalton to Barrow on August 11, 1846, with passenger traffic from the 24th.

By April 1854, the line had been extended east to Ulverston and by the taking over of the Ulverston and Lancaster Railway in 1862, it reached Lancaster. The acquisition of the Whitehaven and Furness Junction Railway in 1865 established its main line around the Cumbrian coast to Whitehaven in the north, connecting with the LNWR at both ends and opening up what had been an extremely isolated part of England.

The FR did not build its own locomotives in its works at Barrow but sourced them from outside manufacturers, no fewer than 15 contractors being used by 1921. Its first locomotive superintendent,

recruited from Bury, Curtis and Kennedy in 1846, was later to be knighted as Sir James Ramsden. However, WF Pettigrew, who took over in 1896 did standardise the locomotive fleet to an extent.

The opening of the Furness Railway led to a mini industrial revolution in the mineral-rich Furness area and led to dramatic expansion of Barrow-in-Furness as an industrial centre. However, with the rundown of traditional industries coming to the area quite early, general manager, Alfred Aslett, transformed the FR into a tourist line, effectively starting the tourist boom in the Lake District.

The FR main line has survived intact and has been a popular route for main line steam railtours, while part of its Lakeside branch was preserved as the Lakeside and Haverthwaite Railway. Even three of its oldest engines survive, although none of its later ones, which were early casualties of LMS standardisation.

0-4-0 No. 3 'Old Coppernob'

THE FR RAN all of its traffic with just four bar-framed 0-4-0s for the first six years of its existence. Built by Bury, Curtis and Kennedy of Liverpool in 1846; one survived shunting in Barrow docks until withdrawal in 1900.

No. 3 had hauled the FR's first passenger train, and on withdrawal, the FR, uniquely among pre-Grouping companies, put No. 3 on display in a glass case on Barrow station. The only surviving Bury bar-framed engine in the UK, it was nicknamed 'Old Coppernob', because of the copper cladding to

its dome-shaped haystack firebox.

It survived a German air raid in the Second World War, although it did receive shrapnel wounds, which can still be seen.

It was put into store for safe keeping in 1941 and after eventual restoration at Horwich works, became one of the exhibits in the Museum of British Transport at Clapham in 1962, moving to the National Railway Museum in 1975. It returned to the Furness peninsula for the 150th anniversary of the FR's first passenger train in 1996.

ABOVE: Furness Railway 0-4-0 No. 3 'Old Coppernob' on display in the National Railway Museum at York.
LEFT: FR 0-4-0 No. 3 on display at Barrow-in-Furness station
THE NOSTALGIA COLLECTION

0-4-0 No. 25

THE SECOND REBUILT ex-FR 0-4-0, which had become Barrow Haematite Steel Co No. 17, was presented by its owners to the Stone Cross Special School in Ulverston in 1960. It was built in 1865 by Sharp Stewart as FR No. 25 and sold in 1873 to the steel company and was converted to a saddle tank.

Again it was purchased privately and moved to Steamtown Carnforth in 1985. Apart from a coat of paint, no work was carried out on the locomotive until its purchase by the late Bert Hitchen, owner of LMS 'Black Five' 4-6-0 No. 45231. Bert made a start on restoring the engine in its later steelworks condition, remaining a saddle tank, but following his death in 2015, the engine's future is unclear.

LEFT: FR 0-4-0ST No. 25 at Carnforth on May 16, 1987.

ABOVE: Furness Railway 0-4-0 No. 20 at the open-air museum at Beamish, Co Durham.

0-4-0 No. 20

A BATCH OF EIGHT 0-4-0 tender locomotives were supplied to the FR between 1863 and 1866, but the line's rapid growth of traffic soon resulted in these small engines becoming redundant and in 1870 the first six of the class were sold to the Barrow Haematite Steel Co, owner of the biggest iron and steel works in the world at that time. The FR kept the other two going until 1918.

Sharp Stewart & Co appears to have converted the six engines to saddle tanks before delivery to the BHSC and they were subsequently rebuilt and overhauled at various times, but with No. 7 uniquely retaining its original 4ft 9in wheel diameter driving wheels.

This engine continued in traffic until 1960, by which time it had given 90 years' service to the steelworks. After just seven years' main line service, along with its other surviving sister, it was presented to a local school. No. 7 stood in the grounds of the George Hastwell Special School in Abbey Road, Barrow for more than 20 years, until it was purchased privately in 1983 and moved to Steamtown at Carnforth in November of that year.

Restoration began, but it was cut short by the death of one of the owners. The Furness Railway Trust acquired the dismantled remains in 1990 to safeguard the future of the locomotive.

On August 24, 1996, the exact 150th anniversary of the first passenger train on the FR, it was announced that the Heritage Lottery Fund had awarded a grant of £97,000 to assist the restoration of No. 20 to its original FR condition. Further grants towards the £140,000 cost of the project were also received.

Copies of the original outline drawings for the locomotive were obtained from the Science Museum and the trust prepared detailed drawings for all the new components required. The frames and motion were delivered to the Barrow-in-Furness workshops of Marconi Marine (VSEL) on December 18, 1996. After a total rebuild,

including the construction of a new boiler, made by Israel Newton & Sons of Bradford, and tender, the locomotive emerged two years later on December 17, 1998, resplendent in FR Indian red livery.

On January 13 1999, No. 20 made its first journey on the Lakeside & Haverthwaite Railway. Lady Grania Cavendish formally relaunched it into service at a ceremony at Haverthwaite on April 20. The oldest working standard gauge steam engine in Britain, No. 20 is regularly operated by the Furness Railway Trust, and has visited many heritage lines, large and small. It is normally now based at either the Ribble Steam Railway or the Locomotion museum at Shildon.

BELOW: Furness Railway 0-4-0 No. 20 departs from Loughborough on the Great Central Railway.

The Furness Railway Trust acquired the dismantled remains in 1990 to safeguard the future of the locomotive.

CHAPTER 11

North Staffordshire Railway

THE NORTH STAFFORDSHIRE Railway was formed to promote lines to serve the Staffordshire Potteries and surrounding areas. Its first passenger train ran on April 17, 1848 from Stoke to Norton Bridge, connecting with the LNWR to Birmingham.

Nicknamed 'The Knotty' and based in Stoke-on-Trent its main routes were constructed between 1846 and 1852 and ran from Macclesfield to Norton Bridge, just north of Stafford on the WCML, and from Crewe to Egginton Junction, west of Derby. These and various branches connected with other companies particularly the LNWR, with its Euston-Manchester expresses using the NSR route via Stoke. In 1913 the NSR was the 18th largest company by route mileage with 216 miles, and perhaps surprisingly, it remained independent, right up to Grouping.

The NSR L class 0-6-2T was developed by JH Adams mainly for coal traffic, but during its early years was also used on expresses between Stoke and Manchester. The class first appeared in 1908 and was so successful that a further 27 followed, the last four appearing just after Grouping. The LMS inherited 196 NSR steam locomotives, the largest being the L class, which were renumbered 2246 to 2273.

Under the LMS standardisation programme all NSR engines had been withdrawn by 1939. Some 0-6-2Ts were sold on withdrawal to collieries, six, LMS Nos. 2253/7, 2262/4 and 2270/1, to Walkden Colliery in Lancashire, later becoming NCB stock. One of these, which had been NSR No. 2 from the 1923 batch and carried the name *Princess* in colliery service, was loaned by the NCB for the city of Stoke-on-Trent's Golden Jubilee Celebrations in 1960. It was sent to Crewe and restored to its NSR condition in madder lake livery, BR sending

ABOVE: LNSR 0-6-2T No. 2 on display at Cheddleton. DAVE FELSTEAD/CVR

'Jinty' 0-6-0T No. 47669 on loan to Walkden to cover for its absence.

No. 2 returned to Walkden where it remained in use until 1966, still in NSR livery, although by then it had been cannibalised along with another engine *Sir Robert*, to make one good one, and although both survived, No. 2 ran on the frames from *Sir Robert* so the engines possibly swapped their identities incorrectly. No. 2 was donated by the NCB to the National Collection and put on loan for display at Shugborough Hall in Staffordshire where it remained until transferred to a new mining museum at Chatterley Whitfield in the Potteries on May 14, 1984. When this closed, it moved to the Churnet Valley Railway at Cheddleton on the one-time NSR Macclesfield-Uttoxeter line on November 18, 1993. Plans to return it to steam stalled and the engine is now on display in the Locomotion museum at

Shildon, still carrying its 1960 paintwork. No. 2 has never steamed in preservation.

Meanwhile *Sir Robert* survived in storage at Walkden until as late as 1969 and was purchased for preservation, but scrap merchants, who had purchased Austerity 0-6-0STs at the site, unfortunately cut up the NSR engine by mistake.

Mersey Railway I class 0-6-4T No. 5 *Cecil Raikes*

THE MERSEY RAILWAY connected Liverpool and Birkenhead via the Mersey Railway Tunnel from 1886 and had four stations. Steam worked, it was extended over the next six years and was the first tunnel under the Mersey and the world's oldest underground railway outside London.

However, steam locomotives were not ideal in the tunnel, passengers did not use it and the railway was bankrupt by 1900; things only changed after electrification in 1903. The Mersey Railway remained independent in 1923, although it became

closely integrated with the LMS electric services in the Wirral and became part of BR in 1948, remaining in use today.

For the opening of the line, eight condensing I class 0-6-4Ts were obtained from Beyer Peacock and these were eventually sold after electrification.

They all found buyers; the first to be sold being No. 5 *Cecil Raikes*, which was bought in 1904 by Shipley Collieries in Derbyshire for £750. The engine's namesake was a Conservative politician, who was a senior member of the

House of Commons, also serving as Postmaster General between 1886 and 1891.

On withdrawal in 1956, *Cecil Raikes* was presented by the NCB to BR and put in store at Derby works. It was then presented by BR to National Museums Liverpool and moved to storage in Liverpool on February 17 that year. It was loaned to Steamport at Southport in 1978 where it was put on display but never restored. Closure of the site led to a move back to storage in Liverpool in 1998 but it remains in store unrestored.

The last four I class

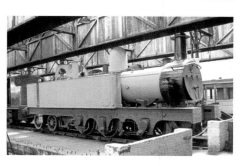

ABOVE: Mersey Railway 0-6-4T No. 5 *Cecil Raikes* still in largely unrestored condition at Steamport Southport on May 18, 1980.

locomotives were sold to J & A Brown Ltd for use on the Richmond Vale colliery line in New South Wales, Australia and No. 1 *The Major* is preserved at the New South Wales Rail Transport Museum in Thirlmere.

North London Railway 75 class 0-6-0T No. 58850

THE NORTH LONDON RAILWAY initially ran from the LTSR's Fenchurch Street station to London's East and West India Docks, opening in 1850. Fifteen years later an extension from Dalston Junction to Broad Street was opened with Broad Street becoming the main terminus, by which time the line had been extended across North London, joining the LNWR but then continuing round west London to join the LSWR's Richmond branch.

Although the LNWR took over the railway's operations on February 1, 1909, the company remained in existence until Grouping. The line was electrified by the LNWR in 1916, and most of the system remains in use today although it is drastically different; the original line is now being used by the Docklands Light Railway.

Thirty of the NLR Class 75 0-6-0Ts designed by JC Park were built at Bow works between 1879 and 1905 for dock shunting and were compact, powerful engines. Some were transferred by the LMS in the 1930s to work on the Cromford and High Peak line in Derbyshire.

No. 58850 was the last of the class to be withdrawn from the C&HP in 1960 and was purchased for preservation. After storage at Derby it arrived on the Bluebell Railway on March 28, 1962. Originally NLR No. 116, the engine became LNWR No. 2650, then LMS No. 7505, later No. 27505 under the LMS renumbering.

ABOVE: NLR 0-6-0T No. 58850 at work on the Bluebell Railway at Freshfield on February 15, 1987.

The NLR tank was one of the locomotives used by contractors for the demolition of the line from East Grinstead to Ardingly in 1964. Although too small for regular service on the Bluebell line it remained active in recent years and was often used on the weekly carriage works shunt at Horsted Keynes.

It even saw service in the rebuilding of line it helped to demolish, the Bluebell's northwards extension back to East Grinstead. Requiring major boiler work, it has been loaned for static display, arriving first at Barrow Hill Roundhouse in January 1999. After a quick visit to the Ecclesbourne Valley Railway at Wirksworth, close to its old stamping ground on the Cromford & High Peak line, it arrived back at Sheffield Park on October 22, 2005, to await its overhaul.

London Tilbury & Southend Railway

79 class 4-4-2T No. 80 *Thundersley*

THE LONDON, TILBURY and Southend Railway was a joint venture between the London and Blackwall Railway and the Eastern Counties Railway, yet surprisingly it did not become part of the Great Eastern Railway.

It opened in 1854, running from Fenchurch Street along the north bank of the Thames to Southend and Shoeburyness. Instead the company worked with the Midland Railway to provide through services and in 1912 it was purchased by the MR.

Thomas Whitelegg, who was born in 1836, was appointed as the locomotive carriage, wagon and marine superintendent of the LTSR at Plaistow works in 1875 after several jobs in the engineering industry, including on the GER. He was responsible for introducing the outside-cylindered 4-4-2T that formed the mainstay of the LTSR's services, replacing engines hired from the GER. The final development was the 79 class of 1909.

The LTSR built only four of this class and when it was taken over by the MR in 1912 lost their green livery and names, however, the MR built more with 10 being delivered in 1923 just after Grouping. The LMS ordered a further 25 and they monopolised LTSR line's suburban workings until superseded by Stanier's three-cylindered 2-6-4Ts.

They survived to be inherited by BR though, which gave them the numbers 41928-41975, and after displacement from the LTS line, they found work on various branches right across the country,

ABOVE: LTSR 4-4-2T No. 80 *Thundersley* in steam in 1956 for the LTSR centenary. COLOUR-RAIL.COM

ABOVE: LTSR 4-4-2T No. 80 *Thundersley* at the Bressingham Steam Museum.

four lasting until 1959.

On March 1, 1856, the LTSR reached Southend with a three-mile extension from Leigh-on-Sea, and the centenary was celebrated in 1956 by BR.

No. 41946, the oldest-surviving member of the 79 class 4-4-2Ts had been displaced from the LTS line and been allocated to Toton by 1953, but was restored by BR to original LTSR green livery as No. 80 *Thundersley*, and it ran from Southend to London on March 3, followed by a public railtour from Bishopsgate on March 11. It was then withdrawn but taken to Derby where it joined other preserved engines rather than being scrapped, and was an obvious choice for eventual designation as part of the National Collection.

It stayed at Derby for many years but on March 17, 1965, along with MR 4-2-2 No. 118 and 2-4-0 No. 158A, *Thundersley* was towed to Hellifield for storage. During March 1967, it moved again from Hellifield to Carnforth to have its dome cut down so it could be towed under WCML wires en route to Preston Park. It returned to Hellifield on August 11 and set off for the south coast on January 19, 1968.

It did not stay long and moved briefly to Attleborough in Norfolk from where it was moved by road to Bressingham Gardens on August 18, 1968. It was restored to steam in 1970 by members of the Norfolk Railway Society led by one-time Norwich shedmaster, Bill Harvey. It has not hauled any more trains since and has been a static exhibit for 40 years.

CHAPTER 12

Caledonian Railway

ABOVE: CR 0-4-4T No. 419 heads a train of two Caledonian coaches near Kinneil on the Bo'ness & Kinneil Railway on July 3, 2004. IAN LOTHIAN

THE CR WAS one of the two major players in Scotland and was formed in the 1830s with the intention of linking Glasgow with the inter-city railways being built in England. Having achieved this by opening to Carlisle in 1849 with routes from Carstairs serving both Glasgow and Edinburgh – the London to Glasgow journey time originally being 12½ hours – it extended its network and soon reached Aberdeen, acquiring a dense network of branch lines in the Glasgow area in the process.

It had been thought that only one Anglo-Scottish route was necessary, but the CR was to find itself competing with the GSWR route and the NBR's Waverley route. However, it was the CR that would partner the LNWR in the principal cross-border services, the carriages being owned jointly as West Coast Joint Stock.

It was not until 1873 that the CR finally obtained a Parliamentary Act to build a railway bridge across the Clyde, and by 1879, the company had built Glasgow Central station and London services were transferred from Buchanan Street.

The Callander and Oban Railway was an independent railway company operated by the CR, giving it access to the West Highlands. The CR was absorbed into the LMS in 1923, and most of its principal routes remain open, a major closure being the section from Dunblane through Callander to Crianlarich.

The CR's locomotive works were at St Rollox, in Springburn, Glasgow. Its early locomotive engineers were Robert Sinclair from 1847 to 1856; Benjamin Connor from

1856 to 1876, and George Brittain from 1876 to 1882.

Better known is Dugald Drummond who served from 1882 to 1890. He was born in Ardrossan on January 1, 1940, his brother Peter also becoming a locomotive engineer. Dugald became foreman erector at the Highland Railway's Lochgorm Works in Inverness under William Stroudley and followed Stroudley to the London Brighton and South Coast Railway before being appointed locomotive superintendent of the North British Railway in 1875.

He designed a variety of engines for the CR but the only survivor is the one-off 4-2-2 No. 123. However, many of his later London and South Western Railway designs were particularly longlived and several survive in preservation.

Hugh Smellie served the CR briefly in 1890, but was quickly succeeded by John Lambie in 1891, who improved on earlier designs, particularly Drummond's 4-4-0s in 1894. Lambie died suddenly on February 1, 1895 and was succeeded by John Farquharson McIntosh, born in 1846 in Farnell, Angus.

Originally an apprentice at the age of 14 with the Scottish North Eastern Railway, which was taken over by the CR in 1866, he progressed through various jobs with the CR, but lost his right hand in an accident. He married Jeanie Fleming Logan, a close relative to author Ian Fleming.

McIntosh's most famous design was the Dunalastair 4-4-0, probably the best-known and mostly highly regarded of the CR's 4-4-0s, yet it didn't survive into preservation. He enlarged it into the 903 Cardean 4-6-0 but these represented little improvement on the Dunalastairs. Two McIntosh locomotives are preserved: a 439 class 0-4-4T and an 812 class 0-6-0. McIntosh died at St Rollox, on February 6, 1918, still working just before his 72nd birthday. The cause of death was never confirmed.

William Pickersgill was born in Nantwich and joined the Great Eastern Railway in 1876. In 1894 he became locomotive superintendent of the Great North of Scotland Railway, and in March 1914 succeeded McIntosh as locomotive, carriage and wagon superintendent of the CR. He further improved on the CR 4-4-0s and introduced 4-6-0s with little more success than his predecessor. In fact the CR's best 4-6-0s were probably the ones it bought from the Highland Railway.

Following the Grouping, Pickersgill was appointed mechanical engineer of the Northern Division of the LMS but retired in 1925. None of his CR designs survived into preservation. The CR handed over 1070 engines to the LMS and 750 of these made it through to Nationalisation in 1948.

4-2-2 No. 123

THE UNIQUE CR Single No. 123 was built in just 66 days by Neilson in 1886, as an exhibition locomotive, winning a gold medal at the Edinburgh International Exhibition in that year. It was used in regular WCML service, often as pilot engine and took part in the Race to the North in 1888. In 1914 it was placed on the CR duplicate list, and renumbered 1123.

The LMS numbered it 14010 and during the 1920s it was allocated to working the directors' saloon, but surprisingly was returned to ordinary service in 1930. The locomotive was withdrawn in 1935, by which time it was the last single-wheeled express engine running in Britain. Even the LMS considered it to be of sufficient historic interest that it set it aside for preservation, although it simply remained in store at St Rollox works.

Restored to steam by BR in 1959 along with three other historic Scottish locomotives, it ran railtours and enthusiast specials until 1964, when it was allocated to Glasgow's Dawsholm shed. After storage at Parkhead shed from October 19, 1964, it moved into the Glasgow Museum of Transport at Pollokshields in June 1966, moving to the new museum at Kelvin Hall in 1987, where it remained until its move to the new Riverside Museum.

ABOVE: LCR 4-2-2 No. 123 + NBR 4-4-0 No. 256 Glen Douglas at Oban with a railtour in May 1962. COLOUR-RAIL.COM

439 class 0-4-4T No. 419

ABOVE: CR 0-4-4T No. 419 in the Rail 150 cavalcade at Shildon on August 31, 1975.

IN 1899, MCINTOSH designed an 0-4-4T for suburban services, followed in 1900 by a larger version, the 439 class. Seventy six were built by the CR, and 16 more by the LMS after 1923.

No. 55189, built at St Rollox in 1909, had worked from Lockerbie, Ardrossan and Edinburgh Dalry Road, then Polmadie from 1952 to 1959, and finally Carstairs, from where it was withdrawn by BR in December 1962. As the last working member of the class, the then recently formed Scottish Railway Preservation Society was keen to save it, but the asking price of £750 proved difficult to raise and only a generous donation by Worcestershire farmer, WEC Watkinson, the society's first president, secured it for preservation.

St Rollox was no longer dealing with steam overhauls; so after restoration at the rival NBR's Cowlairs works to CR blue livery as No. 419, it was delivered to the society's newly acquired Falkirk depot in April 1965, but its first public steaming was not until the autumn of 1971. The CR used air braking but the LMS standardised on vacuum brakes. However, No. 419 retained its air braking, which acts only on the locomotive itself.

No. 419 took part in various open days in Falkirk yard and notably travelled under its own steam in August 1975 to the Rail 150 celebrations at Shildon, together with LNER D49 4-4-0 No. 246 *Morayshire* and three historic SRPS coaches.

The SRPS though, took a long time to find a suitable branch line on which to regularly operate its locomotives, finally settling on nearby Bo'ness, to where the stock was moved in January 1988.

The 0-4-4T was withdrawn in 1992 for a major overhaul, which was completed in March 2001, after which it ran regularly on the Bo'ness & Kinneil Railway, where it is currently undergoing another overhaul.

812 class 0-6-0 No. 828

MCINTOSH'S 812 and 652 classes of 0-6-0 were introduced in 1899, using the same boiler as the Dunalastair, which was held in high regard. Although designed largely for express goods trains, 17 of the 0-6-0s had continuous air brakes and were used on excursion traffic and Clyde Coast boat trains, carrying blue livery. No. 828 was a blue one and initially allocated to Aberdeen.

Ninety six were built in total, all being inherited by the LMS; only three had been withdrawn by 1948. The last one, carrying the BR number 57566 was not withdrawn until 1963 from Ardrossan shed, when it was purchased by the Scottish Locomotive Preservation Trust, which was raising money to purchase selected Scottish engines that had not been nominated for official preservation by the BTC. Unfortunately this was the only engine the trust raised sufficient money to purchase and was not even the trust's first choice, but a CR 4-4-0 had proved

to be too expensive. It had to be immediately removed from BR premises, going first to the ICI explosives factory at Ardeer.

With nowhere to run the engine, it was eventually restored to CR blue livery at Cowlairs works in 1966 as No. 828 and put on display in the Glasgow Transport Museum at Pollokshields in August. However, once the Strathspey Railway had become established, the opportunity was taken to remove the engine from static display and it arrived at Aviemore on October 27, 1980 for a planned return to steam. It was a big job and No. 828 did not haul its inaugural passenger train on the railway until May 15, 1993.

A popular engine, it was withdrawn for overhaul in 2000 and emerged once again on June 14, 2010, with the support of the Heritage Lottery Fund, most work carried out by Strathspey's engineers and volunteers at Aviemore, with Riley & Son doing the boiler work.

Temporarily carrying BR black livery, No. 57566 departs from Boat of Garten on September 15 2000, just before withdrawal for overhaul. DAVE FOWLER

CHAPTER 13

Highland Railway

PARLIAMENT rejected the first proposal to build a railway from Perth to Inverness in 1845 because it was not considered feasible to build or operate a railway across such terrain. The short Inverness & Nairn Railway opened on November 5, 1855 and eventually connected with the Great North of Scotland Railway completing a route from Inverness to Aberdeen, giving Inverness a very circuitous rail link to the south.

The Inverness & Aberdeen Junction Railway opened a new route from Forres to Aviemore over the 1052-ft summit at Dava, connecting with the Inverness & Perth Junction Railway which had succeeded in building a line over the 1484-ft Druimuachdar Pass. The two companies merged on February 1, 1865, becoming the Highland Railway in June, with 242 route miles.

Various companies, together with the Duke of Sutherland, promoted further routes and the Highland Railway's operations extended to Wick and Thurso in the far north, and Kyle of Lochalsh in the west. A shorter route south from Inverness to Aviemore over Slochd summit was completed on November 1, 1898. The direct line was 28 miles shorter than via Forres, reducing the journey time by about an hour.

Much of the 494-mile HR system was single track and crossed inhospitable terrain. Although its shorter branches have closed, most of the HR remains open. One of Scotland's premier heritage lines, the Strathspey Railway runs on part of the original main line north from Aviemore.

In 1865 William Stroudley became the first locomotive supervisor of the new HR, based at Lochgorm works in Inverness. Stroudley designed an 0-6-0T and three were built at Lochgorm, which were the forerunners of the LBSCR 'Terriers'. Even on the HR, Stroudley painted passenger locomotives yellow with crimson frames but goods locomotives were dark green. Stroudley was succeeded by David Jones in 1870.

ABOVE: HR 4-6-0 No. 103 and CR 4-2-2 No. 123 at Dawsholm shed in 1959. PB WHITEHOUSE

Nine 'Skye Bogie' 4-4-0s were built after 1882, but in 1894 Jones introduced the first 4-6-0 to be used in Britain, known as the Jones Goods, and 15 of these were built. After 1885 all locomotives were painted pea green with a darker border, lined with red and white.

Jones was succeeded by Peter Drummond in 1896; the younger brother of Dugald Drummond, he had worked for the LB&SCR, NBR and CR before joining the HR. The first locomotives designed by Drummond were the Small Ben 4-4-0s.

Fredrick Smith followed as locomotive superintendent in 1912, promoted from works manager. Smith designed the River class 4-6-0, which proved much too heavy and were sold to the Caledonian Railway. Christopher Cumming from the NBR took over in 1915, but David Chalmers Urie, son of the LSWR's Robert Urie, briefly took over just before Grouping.

At Grouping 173 assorted HR locomotives were inherited by the LMS but 23 were quickly withdrawn and being non-standard, most followed fairly soon afterwards.

Duke of Sutherland's 0-4-4T *Dunrobin*

SHARP STEWART constructed an 0-4-4T in 1895 for the Duke of Sutherland who built and operated the Sutherland Railway that linked the HR route north from Inverness with the Thurso & Wick Railway, and became jointly owned by the Sutherland Railway and the HR. Peter Drummond's W class was later perpetuated by the HR, the last four engines to be built at Lochgorm works in Inverness.

All four of the 0-4-4Ts passed to the LMS in 1923, and two survived to become BR Nos. 55051 and 55053, the last HR engines in use when withdrawn in 1956-57.

Dunrobin was used by the Duke, running over HR metals until around 1920, but in March

1950, the engine moved under its own steam to the Romney Hythe & Dymchurch Railway in Kent, a journey of more than 745 miles, after which it was placed on static display.

In 1965 the engine and private saloon were exported to Canada, finally finding a home at Fort Steele after purchase by the British Columbian government, where it was used until 2005.

Deemed surplus to requirements, the locomotive was purchased by Beamish museum in County Durham in 2013, and repatriated to Britain. It is currently being overhauled by the SVR at Bridgnorth for eventual use on the running line at Beamish.

ABOVE: 0-4-4T *Dunrobin* at the California State Railway Museum Railfair at Sacramento in May 1991.

I Class 4-6-0 No. 103

THE HIGHLAND Railway's Jones Goods was notable as the first 4-6-0 to run in the British Isles and was the most powerful main line engine in the country at the time. Fifteen were built by Sharp Stewart & Co in Glasgow in 1894. Originally known as the Big Goods class, they became Class 1 under Peter Drummond's 1901 classification scheme.

When the Jones Goods first appeared it was a remarkable advance on anything that Jones, or the HR, had previously built. It had the highest boiler pressure of any British engine to date, of 175psi and the largest outside cylinders. It was also the first HR tender locomotive not to have the then-traditional Allan double frames and inclined cylinders alongside the smokebox.

Although the design was a big success for Jones, he suffered severe scalding in a serious accident involving one of the 4-6-0s and although he recovered, he was permanently affected and by the end of December 1896 ill health had forced his retirement.

The big 4-6-0s were withdrawn between 1929 and 1940, but the first one was considered historically significant enough that

RIGHT: HR 4-6-0 No. 103 in the new Riverside Museum in Glasgow. GLASGOW MUSEUM

even the LMS set it aside for preservation on withdrawal in 1934. Although restored to HR green livery, it remained stored for many years at St Rollox works. It was one of the four Scottish veterans restored to working order by BR in 1959 and spent several years operating enthusiasts' tours. It was incorrectly painted in the original HR Stroudley yellow livery, and based at Glasgow's Dawsholm shed.

During this time, it appeared in the 1965 film Those Magnificent Men in their Flying Machines, partly filmed on the Hitchin to Bedford line, its only visit so far south. It was finally retired in 1964 and stored at Parkhead shed from October that year until put on display in the Glasgow Museum of Transport at Pollokshields in June 1966. It has recently been transferred to the Riverside Museum in Glasgow still in yellow livery.

HR Ben 4-4-0 No. 54398 *Ben Alder*

ABOVE: No. 54398 at Kipps on April 11, 1966. JOHN CRAWLEY

THE HR HAD two Ben classes of 4-4-0s designed by Peter Drummond; the 'Small Bens' and the 'Large Bens' the only difference between them being the size of the boiler. They all survived into LMS service and although the big ones were withdrawn between 1932 and 1937 and the first small one in 1931, 10 survived into BR ownership; No. 54398 *Ben Alder*, lasting until 1953. It went into store at Lochgorm works with talk of it being restored to HR condition, but after being moved round various locations for 14 years including Boat of Garten and eventually Dawsholm in Glasgow, it was eventually cut up in 1967. The powers-that-be had finally decided that it did not justify its place in the National Collection, having been fitted with a Caledonian boiler in LMS days. There are thoughts that its scrapping was in fact a mistake as it was certainly still of sufficient historic interest to have been worthy of private preservation, where it could now be in the unique position of being the only working pre-Grouping Scottish express engine.

Glasgow & South Western Railway 5 class 0-6-0T No. 9

THE GSWR served south-west Scotland from its headquarters at Glasgow St Enoch. The main line between Glasgow and Carlisle via Dumfries, a third alternative route to England, was opened in stages between 1840 and 1850.

The GSWR was formed in 1850 from a merger of the Glasgow, Paisley, Kilmarnock and Ayr Railway and the Glasgow, Dumfries and Carlisle Railway. A number of other companies were absorbed by the GSWR including the Kilmarnock and Troon Railway in 1899; the first railway in Scotland authorised by Act of Parliament, as early as 1808.

In 1921 the GSWR had 1128 route miles in a system that ranged from suburban Glasgow to the wilds of Galloway, with main lines to Stranraer from both Glasgow and Dumfries. Much of the system has survived with the notable exception of the 'Port Road' from Dumfries to Stranraer, and St Enoch station.

Patrick Stirling was the GSWR's first locomotive engineer from 1853 until he left, being succeeded by his younger brother James. Hugh Smellie took over in 1878, having come from the Maryport & Carlisle Railway but

moved on to the CR in 1890. James Manson was the successive appointment, previously having served on the Great North of Scotland Railway, and he was replaced in 1911 by Peter Drummond from the HR.

Robert Harben Whitelegg, born on Merseyside in 1871, had been locomotive superintendent of the London Tilbury and Southend Railway. In 1912 he had produced a large 4-6-4T, but did not join the MR when it took over the LTSR. In 1918 he became locomotive superintendent of the GSWR

BELOW: GSWR 0-6-0T No. 9 on display in the Glasgow Transport Museum at Kelvin Hall.

at Kilmarnock, becoming chief mechanical engineer in 1919.

He designed an even more impressive 4-6-4T for Clyde Coast suburban services from Glasgow but not until 1922. On Grouping he became general manager of Beyer Peacock in Manchester. He died in 1957 having furthered his railway career in the United States.

The GSWR was operated mainly by a variety of typical 4-4-0s and 0-6-0s plus a few 4-6-0s, but traditionally few tank engines. Few survived the LMS pursuit of standardisation in the 1930s and only a single 1 class 0-6-2T became BR stock in 1948. However, one GSWR locomotive did survive; 5 class 0-6-0T No. 9. In 1919 the engine had been reclassified 322, and given the number 324, becoming LMS No. 16379.

It was sold by the LMS in 1934 to a colliery in Denbighshire, passing into NCB ownership. On withdrawal it was presented to the British Transport Commission for preservation, moving to St Rollox works for external restoration in 1965 before being put on display in the Glasgow Museum of Transport at Pollokshields. It has now moved to Riverside.

CHAPTER 14

London Midland & Scottish Railway

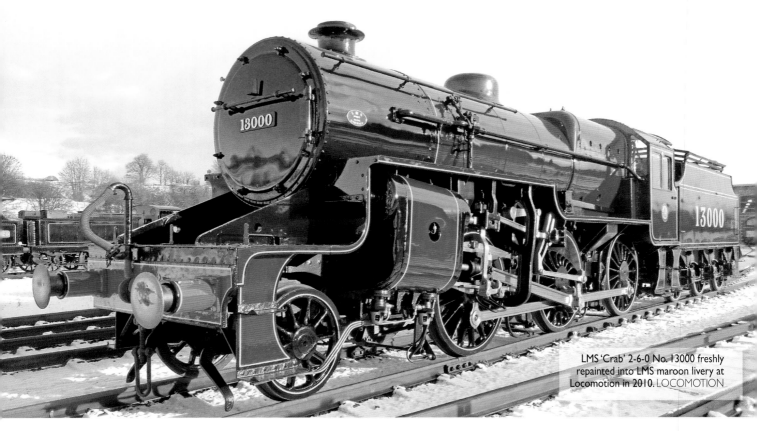

LMS 'Crab' 2-6-0 No. 13000 freshly repainted into LMS maroon livery at Locomotion in 2010. LOCOMOTION

THE LMSR was formed on January, 1923 under the Railways Act of 1921, which grouped more than 120 separate railway companies into just four.

The LMSR was formed of the LNWR including the LYR, MR, CR and HR plus many other smaller companies. Its principal routes were the West Coast Main Line and the Midland Main Line, which had been the main routes of the two largest constituent companies; the LNWR and MR.

The LMS was formed on creation of the Big Four and immediately and simultaneously became the world's largest transport organisation by stock market valuation, the largest commercial undertaking in the British Empire and the UK's second largest employer, beaten only by the Post Office.

The early life of the LMS was initially dominated by MR thinking, in particular the small-engine policy, as a result of the CME and many other senior personnel being of MR background. Even MR locomotive and coach livery prevailed, much to the disgust and disappointment of ex-LNWR staff.

The LMS sat geographically between the GWR and LNER with considerable overlap of territory but there was little overlap with the Southern. A number of lines continued to be jointly owned and operated for several years including the Somerset & Dorset, which came into the LMS in 1930, and the Midland & Great Northern, which went to the LNER as late as 1936.

In 1938, the LMS operated 6870 route miles, excluding its lines in Northern Ireland, but was never particularly profitable. Freight accounted for around 60% of LMS revenue, but competition with the LNER over Anglo-Scottish passenger traffic was fierce with the companies vying to provide the fastest express services. In 1937, the LMS launched the 'Coronation Scot', the last word in luxury express train travel with streamlined locomotives running from Euston to Glasgow Central in 6½ hours.

Competition between the companies culminated in the world steam speed record changing hands several times in the late 1930s until the LNER trounced the LMS Coronation's 114mph with *Mallard*'s 126mph in 1938, a record that still stands.

The locomotive works inherited by the LMS were rationalised, with Crewe and Derby remaining the major players and retaining a considerable degree of autonomy. The L&Y's Horwich works and CR's St Rollox in Glasgow still remained major centres of locomotive construction.

Power classification

THE LMS devised a logical system of power classification for its locomotives, based on tractive effort, following earlier MR practice. A single number from 0 to 9 without a suffix letter was used until 1928 but the suffix P or F began to be used after which a number alone, indicated a mixed-traffic locomotive. Where a mixed-traffic locomotive fell into different power ranges, dual classification was used, e.g. 5P4F. The LMS never built any Class 8 or 9 locomotives, but when Stanier introduced his two designs of 4-6-0 in 1934, it was felt that the two should be in different power classes, although the Jubilee was not the equivalent of a Royal Scot so it was not a Class 6. The designation 5XP was applied to the Jubilees, effectively meaning a Class 5½ passenger engine.

The LMS system was perpetuated by BR although it was not adopted particularly enthusiastically by regions other than the London Midland. The opportunity was taken to make 5X into 6 and revise the higher classifications upwards so the Royal Scots became Class 7 and the Pacifics and 2-8-0s Class 8.

The LMS numbering system

LIKE THE other Big Four companies, the LMS inherited several different haphazard numbering systems from its constituents, with a considerable amount of duplication. The new company was heavily influenced in many ways by MR policy and the MR had introduced a more logical numbering system in 1907 so this was adopted by the LMS, with MR locomotives retaining their old numbers.

The MR system was based on usage, wheel arrangement, power classification, and age, with locomotives of the same class numbered together. The least powerful and oldest classes took the lowest numbers. When the LTSR was absorbed by the MR in 1912, its locomotives were renumbered into this scheme; mostly tank engines, they simply followed on from the MR tank engine numbers.

The LNWR had inherited its numbering system from the Grand Junction Railway, which simply started at No. 1 with no gaps, so a new locomotive would either be numbered at the end of the series or would reuse the number of one that had been scrapped,

although some were put on the 'duplicate' list rather than be scrapped, and this list had various sets of numbers over the years.

Unlike the MR, the GJR and LNWR also named all their passenger tender locomotives and often the names would follow the numbers on to newer replacement engines. In fact, even LNWR freight engines all had names up to 1858 but these were removed from 1863.

The LMS quickly developed its new numbering scheme, which with cases other than the MR, meant that the new number bore no relation to the old one. 1-4999 were MR, plus LTSR and NSR; 5000-9999 were LNWR and NLR; 10000-12999 were L&Y, FR and others; and 14000-17999 were the Scottish railways.

Within these series, the numbers (starting with the oldest in each case) ran in a consistent order; passenger tender, passenger tank, freight tank and freight tender. Somerset & Dorset engines were given numbers in the MR series when the LMS took it over in 1930.

New locomotives built by the LMS did not have a separate series but were fitted

into the appropriate one, which included the vacant 13000 series.

It worked for a while but the LMS policy of standardisation and the rate of new building dictated that the new engines' number series ought to take precedence over those of older ones. So, from 1932, all LMS-built engines were to be put in the number series 1-9999. This did not mean that all pre-Grouping engines would be given five-figure numbers, but when necessary, the oldest engines had 20000 added to their numbers to make space for new engines.

Diesel shunters went into the steam series, but the two main line diesels were given the numbers 10000 and 10001. BR simply added 40000 to nearly all the LMS numbers on Nationalisation and new engines to LMS designs carried on in the same series. The only exceptions were that the few 20XXX numbered engines became 58XXX, main line diesels kept their LMS numbers and diesel shunters went into the 12000 series.

Hughes-Fowler 'Crab' 2-6-0

GEORGE HUGHES had been the last chief mechanical engineer of the L&Y, assuming the role on the LNWR briefly following the 1922 merger and then becoming CME of the LMS in 1923 for just two years.

None of his new designs for the L&Y have survived but he was responsible for the Class 8 four-cylinder express 4-6-0, which was not a successful design as built, and acquired the nickname 'Dreadnought' through its sheer size. However, after drastic rebuilding and the fitting of superheating it became a very capable engine if a bit heavy on coal and was briefly Britain's most powerful express engine until Gresley unveiled his A1 Pacific. The LMS built more of the class, plus a 4-6-4T version, but soon falling victim to the LMS standardisation policy.

On the LMS, Hughes continued to advocate larger and more powerful engines as he had on the L&Y. The LMS could not agree to his express Pacific and heavy-freight 2-8-2 as the cost of new larger turntables would have been prohibitive. However, he quickly designed a powerful mixed-traffic 2-6-0, of which 245 were built between 1926 and 1932 at Horwich and Crewe, and acquired the nickname 'Crabs', because their large cylinders at a pronounced angle created an ungainly appearance.

Despite appearances, it was an advanced design for the time, but it was Hughes' successor, Henry Fowler, who put the class into service. He added one or two Derby touches to the design including a Midland-style tender, which did not match the cab, but the design was too advanced with its smaller MR-style boiler.

This hybrid design proved instantly successful and held its own for many years, even against Stanier's later products; all of the class survived into BR service and some ran until 1967 from Birkenhead shed. Hughes retired in 1925 at the age of 60, and died in 1945.

ABOVE: LMS 'Crab' 2-6-0 No. 2700 approaches Oxenhope on November 3, 1968 on one of its few appearances in steam on the KWVR. JOHN WHITELEY

No. 13000

THE pioneer 'Crab', No. 42700 had been allocated to Mirfield from Nationalisation until 1952, Wakefield in 1955-56, then Bury from 1956 to 1964. After nine months at Gorton, it ended its days at Birkenhead in March 1966. It was selected for official preservation, and on withdrawal, was put into store at Hellifield.

It was placed on loan to the Keighley & Worth Valley Railway shortly before its opening and was towed the short distance to Keighley on June 11, 1968, where, despite its extremely rundown condition, the railway set about putting it back in steam. It hauled its first train on the line in LMS black livery as No. 2700 on October 20, 1968, and performed satisfactorily.

On December 14 that year though, No. 2700 was entrusted with the KWVR's

first Santa special, generally considered to be the first Santa train on any preserved line. The poor engine could not find its feet on the 1-in-58 gradient; taking more than half an hour to get out of Keighley and around 90 minutes to get to Oxenhope. The second run was slightly better but the engine saw very little further service on the line. It went on display at Oxenhope and was returned to BR livery, moving to the NRM on May 20, 1977.

It is surprisingly well travelled, even returning home to Bury in 1996 and Barrow Hill in 1998, before returning to the NRM. Restoration to original condition in LMS maroon livery as No. 13000 was carried out at Locomotion, Shildon in 2010 and it is now back on display at York, with little likelihood of seeing another return to steam.

No. 42765

NO. 13065 WAS built in 1927 and allocated to Kentish Town, moving to Leicester from 1932 to 1935, but then migrating to the North West, before being allocated to Manchester Belle Vue from 1935 to September 1950, Rose Grove for a year, then Fleetwood from August 1951 to May 1964, and finally Birkenhead where many of the class ended their days, being withdrawn from there in December 1966.

Along with No. 42859, it went to Barry scrapyard from where it was rescued by Andy Wilson and moved to the KWVR in April 1978. Midway through its restoration it moved to Derek Foster's works at Kirby on Merseyside in 1990, but on completion of its restoration it moved again to the ELR on August 14, 1993. Here it returned to steam in September that year, in BR black livery, unfortunately just missing the railway's big gala celebrating the 25th anniversary of the end of BR steam.

However, after working just one train on September 26, an acrimonious dispute developed between the owner and the railway, which had acquired a one third share in the engine.

Claiming that Andy Wilson owed the railway money for the restoration, the engine was withdrawn from service by the railway and Wilson made a counterclaim in court for custody of the 'Crab', which was ultimately resolved only by the railway acquiring the other two-thirds share in it.

Immediately popular with enthusiasts when it finally entered traffic in early 2004, this was the right engine working on the right line and the first of its class to work in regular service in the preservation era.

Withdrawn in July 2003 after 10 years' service including many visits to other heritage lines, the engine was overhauled once more by the railway and returned to service in 2013, now resplendent in LMS maroon livery as No. 13065.

RIGHT: LMS 'Crab' 2-6-0 No. 42765 heads a goods train past Irwell Vale on the ELR on February 22, 1994.

No. 42859

NO. 13159 WAS a north-western engine from new in 1928, working from Longsight and other sheds, until it settled at Stockport Edgeley from September 1950 to February 1959. A move south saw it at Willesden from February 1959 to March 1962, a brief spell at Nuneaton, then Birkenhead from June 1962 to be withdrawn in December 1966 after which it was sent to Woodhams at Barry.

It was not until December 1986 that it was purchased and moved by its new owner to Hull Dairycoates. Closure of that site saw nearly all stock including the dismantled No. 42859, transferred to the former RAF base at Binbrook in Lincolnshire in 1995.

Little further progress was made and the

engine was effectively 'lost' until a bitter dispute surfaced in 2012. It appeared that the driving wheels and tender frame had been removed in respect of non-payment of rent. The boiler and frames though were removed from Binbrook under police supervision and moved to a secret location, while legal proceedings for the return of the wheels and tender frame were commenced. However, the boiler was cut up in a Nottingham scrapyard having been sold by the owner.

While it would be possible for a new boiler to be constructed, the lack of progress towards any meaningful restoration over the past 29 years would suggest that this is unlikely in the foreseeable future.

BELOW: The dismantled No. 42859 at Binbrook. ROBIN JONES

CHAPTER 15

Sir Henry Fowler

SIR HENRY FOWLER had an enviable record for locomotive design on the MR but after Grouping he was appointed deputy CME of the LMS, under the L&Y's George Hughes. Nevertheless he quickly took over as CME in October 1925.

Fowler tends to be blamed for the MR's famous small-engine policy being adopted by the LMS, but in fact Fowler agreed with his predecessor Hughes that more power was needed. Fowler never had the authority on the LMS that his position merited and Anderson, a Midland man who was in charge of motive power, ensured that his opinions prevailed and

the LMS continued the production of various MR standard designs, with some modifications, including the Compound 4-4-0, 2P 4-4-0, 4F 0-6-0, and 3F 0-6-0T.

As train loads increased, the small-engine policy became increasingly inappropriate and in 1928, the LMS realised that a big express engine was required for WCML expresses, to compete with the LNER, and Fowler introduced the Royal Scot 4-6-0, based closely on the SR Lord Nelson. He also designed the 7F 0-8-0, 'Big Bertha' the Lickey banker 0-10-0, and the Beyer-Garratt 2-6-0+0-6-2. The latter were really just two small engines

bolted together and suffered from the drawback of undersized axleboxes and the short-travel valves, which afflicted MR designs almost to the end of BR steam.

Sir Henry retired in 1931 and died seven years later; his Midland designs have fared well in preservation but his LMS designs have not. Many 3F 0-6-0Ts and three 4F 0-6-0s, mostly of LMS construction, found their way to Barry scrapyard, and being of very basic design have proved popular with restoration groups, while the type of use they experience on heritage lines does not stretch the inadequate design features to the extent that main line service used to.

BELOW: MR 3F 'Jinty' 0-6-0T No. 47279 departs from Oakworth on the KWVR.

No. 47279

THE OLDEST SURVIVING 'Jinty', was built by Vulcan Foundry at Newton-le-Willows in 1924 and was originally numbered 7119. It shunted at Toton yard for many years until renumbered 7279 in 1934 and transferred to Nottingham shed. In 1938 it was transferred to Wellingborough, where it stayed until 1957, and worked from Bedford from August of that year until July 1963 when it moved north to Workington. It was finally withdrawn from Sutton Oak on Merseyside in December 1966 and was sold to Woodham's scrapyard at

Barry in South Wales.

No. 47279 was purchased privately for use on the Keighley & Worth Valley Railway, arriving by road in August 1979. Restoration took eight years but it was returned to steam in December 1987 and became a popular, reliable and authentic engine on the former MR branch. It returned to steam after another overhaul in the summer of 2001 but its 10-year boiler certificate expired in 2011 and the engine is on display at Oxenhope awaiting its turn in the queue for overhaul.

LMS 3F 0-6-0T

THIS NUMEROUS, popular and longlived class of engine was based on Fowler's MR rebuilds of Johnson's 2441 class of 1899, featuring a Belpaire firebox and improved cab. Four-hundred and twenty-two were built between 1924 and 1930, and were popularly known as 'Jinties'. The class was one of several MR designs perpetuated with little modification by the LMS for several years. While some were built at Horwich, many were built by contractors.

This huge class was naturally spread across the entire LMS network, including joint lines such as the S&D and M&GN, and although primarily shunting engines, their earlier years saw them on some demanding passenger duties such as suburban trains from Broad Street to North London. The last survived in BR service right up to 1967.

Seven 'Jinties' from North Western sheds found their way to Barry scrapyard and all have been returned to service. In addition, one was bought straight out of BR service and another from the NCB after industrial service, but the last one, No. 47564 was a derelict hulk, which had been used as a stationary boiler and is unlikely to steam again.

No. 7298

THIS 'JINTY' is one of a batch built by Hunslet in Leeds, entering service as No. 7138 in November 1924, and allocated to Camden, but serving from several sheds in the southern part of the LNWR system until August 1954 when as BR No. 47298, it moved north to Sutton Oak shed, near St Helens.

Overhauls were carried out at Derby works or sometimes the former NLR works at Bow, and the engine carried nine different boilers during its working life, including a brand-new one in 1938.

Withdrawal came in December 1966 and like No. 47279, the engine was sold to

Woodhams at Barry. It escaped from the scrapyard earlier though, purchased by Derek Foster and moving to Steamport at Southport on July 27, 1974, returning to steam in August 1979. It had the honour of making an appearance at the nearby Rocket 150 cavalcade at Rainhill in 1980.

The closure of Steamport saw a move to the Llangollen Railway in 1984 where it saw occasional use, then the East Lancashire Railway from May 1988, where it was the line's first operational main line locomotive. It was moved to its owner's works at Kirby in 1990 for overhaul, returning to Llangollen

on June 25, 1991, where it has seen regular service, though often in Thomas blue livery, which has made it popular for hire to other railways for Days out with Thomas events. The engine is currently undergoing a heavy overhaul at Llangollen.

ABOVE: LMS 3F 'Jinty' 0-6-0T No. 7298 passes Burrs on the East Lancashire Railway during the early days of the line's reopening on April 9, 1989.

No. 47324

NO. 16407 WAS built by North British at Glasgow, entering service at the former Caledonian shed at Dawsholm, in June 1926. In 1931 it was transferred to Ayr for use as station pilot and other duties but in August 1933, was transferred to Edge Hill shed (8A) at Liverpool, then to nearby Speke Junction (8C) where it received the number 7324.

A move across the Mersey to Birkenhead came in 1939, where it worked for 27 years until withdrawal in 1966. It was hauled to Barry scrapyard with another 'Jinty', No. 47406 and two 'Crab' 2-6-0s; Nos. 42765 and 42859.

Rescue came when No. 47324 was bought by the Fowler 3F Society and moved to the Mid-Hants Railway on February 7, 1978 for restoration. In May 1986, the engine was moved again, to the Avon Valley Railway near Bristol.

The society and its engine finally settled on a permanent home on the East Lancashire Railway on September 22, 1992, and with much of the cost of restoration met by the railway, No. 47324 first ran on March 14, 2005 and entered ELR service on April 2.

RIGHT: LMS 'Jinty' 0-6-0T No. 47324 crosses Summerseat viaduct with a goods train on the East Lancashire Railway on January 29, 2006.
PAUL CHANCELLOR

No. 47327

NO. 16410 WAS built in Glasgow in 1926 by North British and originally allocated to Motherwell shed (66B). It was well travelled and worked from various other sheds, including Cricklewood (14A) from 1934, Willesden (1A), Carlisle Upperby (12B), Brunswick (27F), Derby (17A) and Walton (27E). Withdrawn from service from Aintree in December 1966, it was sold to Woodham Brothers in 1967, but bought by the Midland Railway Trust in 1970 and moved to Derby in the July. Moving to Butterley in February 1975, it was the second 'Jinty' to be returned to steam there, entering service in January 1992.

It is now owned by Derby City Museums and Art Gallery and is on long-term lease to the Midland Railway Trust. It has run in BR livery as No. 47327, both LMS black and maroon as No. 16410, in Thomas blue, and from 2013 in Somerset & Dorset Prussian blue livery as No. 23.

RIGHT: IN SDJR blue livery, 3F 0-6-0T No. 23 is seen at Swanwick Junction on the Midland Railway-Butterley on May 6, 2013. ALAN WEAVER

No. 47564

THE NEWEST 'surviving' 'Jinty', No. 16647 was built in 1928 by Hunslets and worked from Devons Road (1D), Barrow (11A), Workington (11B) and Lostock Hall (24C), until withdrawal in 1965. However, it saw further use as a stationary boiler for carriage heating at Red Bank carriage sidings near Manchester Victoria, where it was still in existence, though in a derelict state as late as 1972.

The remains were recovered and moved to Derby in May 1972 as a source of spares for the Midland Railway Trust's three other 'Jinties'.

Moved to Butterley in February 1975, it is owned by Derby City Museums and Art Gallery and is on long-term lease to the Midland Railway Trust, but what little is left of the engine is unlikely ever to be restored in its own right.

No. 47383

BUILT IN 1926 at Vulcan Foundry, in BR days No. 47383 worked from Chester until June 1961, moving to Speke Junction for 18 months then Rose Grove from June 1963 to January 1966. From then until December 1966, the engine worked from Newton Heath.

It was one of the last of the class in BR service, which had its life extended through being hired to the NCB to work at Williamthorpe colliery in Nottinghamshire, from February to September 1967; it was officially allocated to Westhouses.

The only 'Jinty' to be purchased straight out of BR service, it was bought by the Manchester Rail Travel Society on withdrawal. The engine was moved to the SVR on May 26, 1968, but it was fairly run down and proved no easier to return to service than engines that had stood at Barry for years. However, it was returned to steam in early 1974 and proved a useful and popular member of the railway's fleet for many years although it is currently again in need of overhaul and is on display in the Engine House at Highley.

ABOVE LEFT: LMS 3F 'Jinty' 0-6-0T No. 47383 climbs Eardington bank on the SVR on May 29, 1989.

No. 47406

NO. 16489 WAS built by Vulcan Foundry at Newton-le-Willows in 1926 and after spending a few weeks at nearby Warrington, made its first home at Crewe South shed, from where it mainly shunted Basford Hall sidings and the carriage sheds. In October 1928 it moved to Carnforth where it spent almost 32 years, being renumbered 7406 in the general LMS renumbering.

After 1960 No. 47406 changed shed a number of times; returning to Warrington (Dallam) until 1962, Workington for a few months, then the GCR shed at Gorton, Manchester until January 1965, and finally finishing its days at Liverpool Edge Hill, from where it was withdrawn in December 1966. It ended up in Barry scrapyard the following July, its longest-ever journey away from the North West.

Of the seven 'Jinties' at Barry, No. 47406 was the last to leave. Being small, simple locomotives they were ideal restoration projects and the first two, Nos. 47327 and 47357 left in 1970, in relatively complete condition. But No. 47406 had inevitably been stripped for spares and all that was left of it were the frames, cylinder block, wheels, boiler and a little rusty platework.

It moved initially to the Peak Rail headquarters in Buxton in June 1983, but when Peak Rail moved from its Buxton site, the locomotive was sold to Roger Hibbert, who moved it to the Great Central Railway, where he was already working on his 8F 2-8-0 No. 48305. The 'Jinty' arrived at Quorn & Woodhouse on December 21, 1989, and once the 8F restoration was completed, No. 47406 was moved into Loughborough shed.

It was a huge job, which would have been considered a 'project impossible' in early preservation days, but the locomotive was returned to traffic on January 30, 2010, proving a very useful addition to the fleet, while often being seen on visits to other heritage lines.

ABOVE: LMS 3F 0-6-0T No. 47406 departs from Loughborough on the GCR in January 2010. DAVE WILSON

ABOVE: LMS 'Jinty' 0-6-0T No. 16440 in LMS maroon livery at Butterley on May 30, 1982.

No. 16440

NO. 16440 WAS built by North British in Glasgow in 1926 and first allocated to Devons Road, but quickly moved to Willesden (1A), then to Liverpool Edge Hill (8A) as BR No. 47357 in 1950. Withdrawn in 1966 and sold to Woodham Bros, it was purchased along with No. 47327 by the Midland Railway Trust in 1970 and moved to Derby on July 18 for restoration work, returning to steam in June 1973, the last steam engine to be overhauled at Derby.

Moved to Butterley in February 1975, it was the first main line locomotive to work there, in LMS crimson lake livery as No. 16440.

Although the engine adopted authentic BR black livery as No. 47357 after it was joined in service by No. 47327, both engines reverted to LMS identities in 2000, with No. 16440 in its non-authentic maroon guise and No. 16410 in LMS black.

After regular use at what became the Midland Railway-Butterley, the engine was withdrawn for a major overhaul, now owned by Derby City Museums and Art Gallery and long-term lease to the Midland Railway Trust. The 47357 Jinty Appeal was formed in early 2011, by Marcello Gabrielli, to raise funds for the overhaul of the engine.

No. 47493

BUILT IN 1927, No 16576 was allocated to the North London Railway shed at Devons Road, Bow, where it stayed until September 1954, when it moved to Speke Junction on Merseyside for eight years, apart from a short spell at Newton Heath. From July 1962 to September 1965, it worked from Springs Branch but ended its days at Edge Hill in December 1966.

Purchased from Barry scrapyard by Barry Buckfield, the engine moved first to Radstock on November 25, 1972, then on to the East Somerset Railway on November 18, 1973 when David Shepherd acquired his base at Cranmore.

Returned to steam in July 1976, the engine worked the ESR reopening train on April 4, 1980 and worked there for many years but moved to Tunbridge Wells West in 1999 for boiler work that could not be undertaken at Cranmore. It was not the intention for it to work regularly on the Spa Valley Railway but a change of policy saw it remain there, returning to steam on October 12, 2003. It has recently been withdrawn for another overhaul, which will take place at Tunbridge Wells West, with a speedy return to service expected.

ABOVE: LMS 3F 0-6-0T No. 47493 at Groombridge on the Spa Valley Railway on September 9, 2010. NICK GILLIAM

No. 47445

NO. 16528 WAS built in 1927 by Hunslet in Leeds and worked in the Crewe area for all its LMS and BR career, at Alsager until July 1960. On withdrawal from Crewe South in April 1966 though, No. 47445 was sold by BR to Hargreaves (West Riding) Ltd for use at its Crigglestone opencast coal disposal point, near Wakefield, where it carried an orange livery.

It was perhaps inevitably acquired for preservation when it became available in June 1970, arriving at Derby on July 15, 1970 and moving with the two ex-Barry 'Jinties' to Butterley in February 1975.

No. 47445 was dismantled and undergoing heavy repair in the shed at Swanwick Junction, owned by Derby City Museums and Art Gallery and on long-term lease to the Midland Railway Trust.

ABOVE: LMS 4F 0-6-0 No. 44123 at Barry scrapyard on February 15, 1975.

No. 44123

NO. 4123 WAS constructed at Crewe in August 1925 and sent to Willesden shed. The locomotive moved several times in the next 25 years until settling at Barnwood, Gloucester in September 1950 for most of the rest of its working life. As a Gloucester engine in BR days No. 44123 was a regular visitor to the Bristol and Bath area, and would have passed through Bitton station many times during its working life.

The end came for the engine in June 1965 when it was condemned and sold to Woodham Brothers in September of that year. It was to languish there until December 1981 when it was moved to the Mid Hants Railway, moving again five years later to the Avon Valley Railway at Bitton, arriving on May 20, 1986. Since then, restoration of the engine has progressed well. Some of the work carried out so far includes a new cab, footplate and dragbox, boiler cladding and brake gear, while a collection of spare parts has also been made or purchased. Work is also taking place on the tender, with the intention of fabricating a new top half to be united with the restored chassis.

ABOVE: LMS 4F 0-6-0 No. 44123 in 1987, six years after arrival at Bitton.
R LEITCH/PAUL CHANCELLOR

4F 0-6-0

THE 4F WAS Fowler's LMS development of his own 197-strong MR 3835 class of 1911, with only a few modifications, mainly being left-hand drive.

The LMS built 530 4Fs between 1923 and 1928, continuing the MR number series from 4027. The MR engines were notorious for their inadequate axlebox bearings, and the LMS 4F inherited this design weakness, yet as late as 1937, William Stanier was persuaded by the operating department to authorise 45 more to be built.

The simple design was considered generally successful and proved longlived though and a few worked for BR right up to 1966.

No. 4027

THE FIRST of the LMS-designed engines were allocated to Bushbury in early BR days, moving to Bescot from 1959-1963. Withdrawn from Workington shed in November 1964, it had been nominated for official preservation as part of the National Collection and was put into storage in the MR shed at Hellifield.

It was moved to the closed shed at Leicester on January 9, 1968, with a view to it being put on display in a new museum in the city, but this did not materialise and it moved again to the new National Collection store at Preston Park in September 1970.

It didn't stay long and returned to Leicester in August 1972, but remained in store until being sent on loan to the Midland Railway Centre at Butterley in 1975. It was returned to steam in December 1979 and worked on the line for several years, gaining a main line certificate to enable it to participate in the Rocket 150 cavalcade at Rainhill in May 1980. It made further trips out, appearing regularly at BR open days at Coalville.

It moved to the Gloucestershire Warwickshire Railway in 2009 where a heavy overhaul is in progress at Toddington.

ABOVE: LMS 4F 0-6-0 No. 4027 heads a demonstration coal train at a BR open day at Mantle Lane depot, Coalville on June 5, 1983.

BELOW: No. 4027 works a short MGR coal train at the CEGB's Castle Donington power station on June 23, 1985.

ABOVE: LMS 4F 0-6-0 No. 44422 passes Berwyn with a goods train on the Llangollen Railway in October 2008.

No. 44422

NO. 4422 was built at Derby in 1927, being first allocated to Leicester shed on October 26 but transferred to Wigston in January 1929.

Moving to Bristol in 1940 and then Bath Green Park in 1948, BR No. 44422 spent the rest of its working life in south-west England, frequently working on the Somerset and Dorset line and piloting West Country Pacifics or Standard 9F 2-10-0s across the Mendip Hills on holiday specials.

Tablet gear was fitted during its life on the S&D and the engine is unique in being the only left-hand drive 4F in preservation.

Its final BR overhaul was at Horwich and No. 44422 was withdrawn from Gloucester shed in June 1965 and quickly moved to Woodham's scrapyard at Barry. A team of preservationists from the North Staffordshire Railway Society raised £4860 to buy it for restoration at Cheddleton on what was to become the Churnet Valley Railway; the 87th of 212 steam locomotives to leave the scrapyard, moving by road in April 1977.

No. 4422 was returned to steam during September 1990, and although used regularly on the CVR, was often hired out to other lines, sometimes for long periods, particularly the East Lancashire Railway in the 1990s and more recently the Nene Valley Railway. It received a full overhaul in 2004, assuming its BR identity as No. 44422, but after expiry of its boiler certificate moved to Peak Rail at Rowsley for its next overhaul. However, in a rapid about-turn, the 4F has moved again, to the West Somerset Railway with a long-term operating agreement after completion of its overhaul.

ABOVE: No. 44422 passes Castor on the Nene Valley Railway in January 2012.

LEFT: No. 44422 undergoing restoration at Cheddleton on the Churnet Valley Railway on May 18, 1980.

NCC U2 4-4-0 No. 74 *Dunluce Castle*

THE NORTHERN Counties Committee's U2 4-4-0s showed a strong MR influence in their design and resembled the LMS 2P 4-4-0s, but their principal dimensions were quite different meaning that they weren't simply an Irish equivalent of the 2P.

The NCC was owned by the LMS and operated trains in Ulster. Eighteeeen U2s were built between 1924 and 1937, the first 10 by North British and they worked the top-link expresses up to 1950. The last to be withdrawn, in June 1962, was No.74 *Dunluce Castle*, which was restored to LMS (NCC) livery at the UTA's Duncrue Street workshops and in April 1963 was transferred to the Belfast Transport Museum. It can now be seen in the Ulster Folk and Transport Museum at Cultra, Co Down.

Patriot 4-6-0 No. 45551 *The Unknown Warrior*

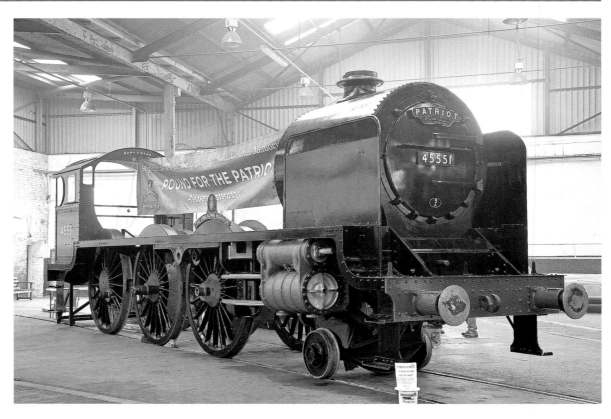

RIGHT: Patriot 4-6-0 No. 45551 *The Unknown Warrior.* FRED KERR

THE THREE-CYLINDERED 4-6-0s introduced towards the end of Sir Henry Fowler's reign as CME, were built between 1930 and 1934. The class members were nominally rebuilds of Bowen-Cook's large-boilered LNWR Claughton 4-6-0 and the first two were produced from the remains of two Claughtons badly damaged in accidents. Little of these engines was actually reused, basically just driving wheels, bogies and a few standard fittings.

Nicknamed 'Baby Scots', but officially known as Patriots after 1937, they were a small-boilered version of Fowler's Royal Scot, with a similar chassis combined with a Derby-designed boiler as used on the rebuilt Claughtons.

The next 40 were also nominally rebuilds of Claughtons, retaining the same numbers; the rebuilding generally considered to be more of an accounting exercise. They were all renumbered 5500-41 in 1934 but the last 10 were classified as new builds and numbered 5542-51. Another five were ordered, but William Stanier ordered his taper boiler to be fitted and they became the first five Jubilees, numbered from 5552, and initially not the equal of a Patriot.

Patriot names were in no logical pattern, some retaining Claughton names; some continuing various themes, with seven never being named at all. Between 1946 and 1948, 18 Patriots were rebuilt with Stanier taper boiler plus cab and tender, again as paper rebuilds, but this did not make them identical to new Jubilees.

The original engines were fitted with smoke deflectors from new but the taper boiler engines did not carry them at first, though from 1948 they were fitted with Stanier Royal Scot-type deflectors.

The remaining parallel-boilered Patriots survived into the 1960s, long enough to become favourites with enthusiasts, this despite being heavily outnumbered by Stanier products. However, all the Patriots were withdrawn between 1960 and 1965, and none survived into preservation.

In 2007 a proposal to build a new Fowler Patriot, using the surviving drawings was announced, leading to the formation of a limited company with charitable status. The Patriot is undoubtedly a big gap in the story of LMS express power.

The intention is to create a new Royal British Legion-endorsed national memorial engine, and No. 45551 will be named *The Unknown Warrior*, hopefully completed in time for the 100th anniversary of the Armistice in 2018.

The new national memorial engine is taking shape quickly at Llangollen and will be a unique contribution to the 2018 Armistice Day Centenary commemorations, and a permanent memorial to all fallen servicemen.

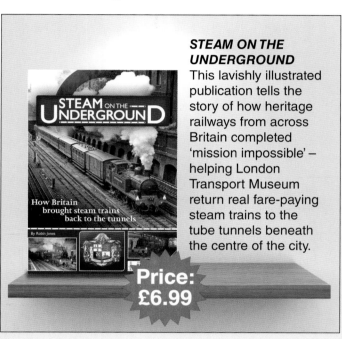
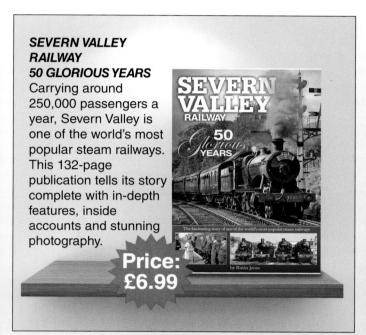

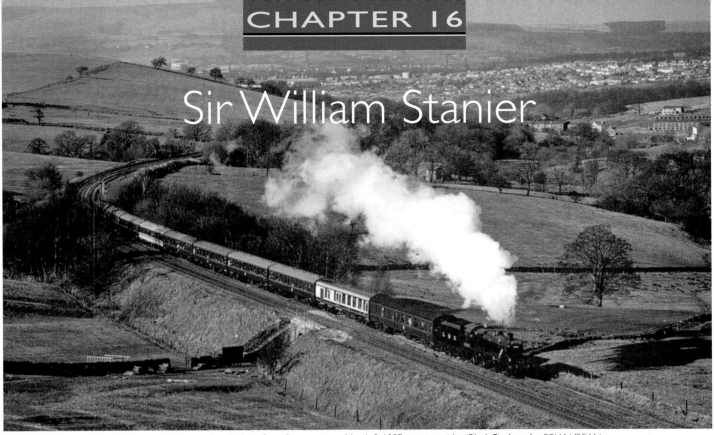

CHAPTER 16

Sir William Stanier

ABOVE: LMS mogul No. 2968 passes Cliviger on the climb to Copy Pit summit on March 8, 1997, running with a 'Black Five' tender. BRIAN DEAN

SIR HENRY FOWLER retired in 1931, and Ernest Lemon became CME very briefly until William Stanier was head-hunted from the GWR, a move which was to transform locomotive development on the LMS and influence British locomotive design right up to the end of steam. Stanier was born in Swindon, where his father was William Dean's chief clerk.

Stanier followed his father into a career with the GWR in 1891, and from 1897 was a draughtsman, before becoming inspector of materials three years later. In 1904, GJ Churchward appointed him as assistant to the divisional locomotive superintendent in London. Further promotions followed and Stanier became works manager at Swindon in 1920.

After his move to the LMS on January 1, 1932, Stanier resolved to stamp out the locomotive department's internal conflicts. His brief was to introduce modern and more powerful locomotive designs, which inevitably saw a move towards Swindon tradition. He naturally reversed the small-engine policy inherited from the MR, and his designs for the LMS included the numerous 'Black Five' 4-6-0s and 8F 2-8-0s, the Jubilee express 4-6-0s and the Princess Royal and Princess Coronation Pacifics, the latter being the most powerful express engines in Britain at the time.

His engines have a neat, distinctive but stylish appearance, with Swindon's influence recognisable in the basic outline but without the traditional GW details. The fitting of hooters rather than traditional whistles still make Stanier's locomotive products instantly recognisable long before they come into view.

Knighted during the war, Stanier worked as a consultant for the Ministry of Supply and retired in 1944. He died in Rickmansworth in 1965.

Being such successful and longlived designs, Stanier's products have fared extremely well in preservation; virtually none of his traditional steam designs have been rendered extinct, with many classes represented in considerable numbers in preservation.

2-6-4T No. 2500

STANIER'S 4P three-cylinder 2-6-4T was designed to work on the London Tilbury and Southend line where the additional power of the three cylinders was required to accelerate the heavy suburban trains between frequent stops. Thirty-seven were built in 1934 at Derby, before Stanier switched to a two-cylinder version in 1935, more suited to slightly less onerous tasks.

The first of the class No. 42500 was nominated in 1960 to represent the 2-6-4T design in the National Collection, though it was not one of Stanier's better-known designs. Withdrawal followed quickly as the LTS line was electrified.

Initially stored at Derby works, it moved to Stratford in 1965 and on to Preston Park in March 1968. December 1968 though, saw better news when it was moved to Bressingham where not only was it on view to the public but it was returned to steam in 1971, resplendent in LMS lined black livery.

However, it has never hauled a train in preservation and moved to the NRM at York in July 1997. It is thought that not much work would be needed to put it in steam again and there have even been serious proposals by the museum to put it to work on the main line.

ABOVE: LMS Stanier 2-6-4T No. 2500 on display in the National Railway Museum at York.

2-6-0 No. 42968

STANIER'S CLASS 5 2-6-0, normally known as Stanier moguls, were Stanier's first products for the LMS. They were designed at Horwich, basically as a development of the Hughes-Fowler 'Crab' 2-6-0, and all 40 were built at Crewe between October 1933 and March 1934.

The main change to the design was the adoption by Stanier of a taper boiler, as was standard on the GWR and used on the very similar Churchward 4300 class mogul. There is a story that Horwich works was so keen to please the new boss that the first engine was given a GWR style top-feed cover. Apparently Stanier was not impressed and it was quickly removed.

Using a higher boiler pressure than on the 'Crabs', it therefore managed with smaller cylinders, so these were positioned more traditionally than on the Hughes' design, but the engines were still provided with a narrow Fowler tender.

The original numbers 13245-13284 changed in the 1933 renumbering to 2945-2984, following on from the 'Crabs'. Stanier quickly followed the moguls with a larger mixed-traffic 4-6-0, although no more moguls were built withdrawals did not start until November 1963 and the last one remained in service right up to February 1967. Being relatively few in number, they were concentrated mostly in the North West but were seen at times on most parts of the LMS system.

No. 2968 was allocated new to Willesden, moving to Edge Hill in April 1935, then Crewe in February 1942, from where it worked from North or South shed until June 1961, when it moved to Birkenhead. After a year at Nuneaton in 1961-62, it was reallocated to Springs Branch where, apart from spending six months at Heaton Mersey and a year at Mold Junction, it worked until withdrawal in December 1966.

The last survivor of its class, No. 42968 was purchased by Dai Woodham and found its way to Barry scrapyard. It was a natural choice for preservation, and was bought by the Stanier Mogul Fund and moved by rail to the Severn Valley Railway on December 13, 1973.

It was December 1990 before it was returned to steam, in LMS lined black livery as No. 2968, but it quickly became one of the railway's most popular locomotives, also seeing extensive and very successful main line operation, though this was using a Stanier 'Black Five' tender.

A further overhaul was completed in 2002 with the engine appearing in BR livery for the next 10 years, though further main line use was precluded as vital paperwork had disappeared. Nevertheless, the engine was always a popular attraction on regular visits to other heritage lines. A third overhaul is now in progress.

ABOVE: In LMS lined black livery, LMS Stanier mogul No. 2968 starts the climb of Eardington bank at Hay Bridge on the SVR on April 12, 1992.

ABOVE: No. 42968 crosses Oldbury viaduct near Bridgnorth on the Severn Valley Railway in April 2003.

'Black Five' 4-6-0

IN THE 1930s, the LMS still had many diverse, often ancient locomotives inherited from its various constituents, including a great number of engines of Midland heritage, many actually built during Fowler's tenure as the LMS CME. Inevitably the company wanted to standardise, and a modern, powerful, standard mixed-traffic engine was a big priority.

Stanier came up with two similar designs more or less simultaneously. The Class 5 and the 5XP 4-6-0s. The Class 5s were painted black and became known as 'Black Fives' while the maroon 5XPs became known as Jubilees after the pioneer class member No. 5552 named *Silver Jubilee* (and which, uniquely, was also black).

The 'Black Five' was introduced in 1934, very similar in size and power to the GWR Hall, with two cylinders, a taper boiler and 6ft driving wheels. In a class built over a 16-year period and that would eventually number 842, there were inevitably many detail variations, some of which were fairly drastic in later days.

Their numbering was complicated and although Crewe was supposed to build the first 20, Nos. 5000-5019, the next 50 were ordered from Vulcan Foundry and these were all delivered before Crewe finished its first one. As well as Vulcan, 227 were built by Armstrong Whitworth and naturally Derby works eventually joined in from 1943.

Eventually, the 500th engine, No. 5499, entered service but the numbering block was full as No. 5500 was already the first of the Patriot 4-6-0s. The next 200 'Black Fives' were numbered from 4800 to 4999, but even this was not enough and the last batch, built in BR days, took the BR numbers 44658 to 44799. As the 4F 0-6-0s were numbered up to 44657 it was perhaps fortunate that no more 'Black Fives' were needed as BR was by then designing its very similar Standard 5MT 4-6-0.

Early detail differences were demonstrated in the size and shape of boilers, so they were not interchangeable but later engines built during Ivatt's reign as CME even had a four-inch longer wheelbase. Ivatt also tried steel fireboxes and double chimneys. No. 44767 had Stephenson valve gear, 20 others had Caprotti valve gear and the last two, Nos. 44686 and 44687, built at Horwich in 1951, had a different type of Caprotti valve gear, later to be used on some BR Standard 5MTs.

Four 'Black Fives' were named, all Scottish regimental names. The class was seen the length and breadth of the LMS system and after Nationalisation, they spread their wings even further, often being seen on holiday specials to the East Coast and even on the Southern Region. Changes to BR regional borders also saw the class move into traditional GWR or LNER depots in the 1960s. No. 45401 was the first withdrawal, in 1961 after accident damage, but the last ones were not withdrawn until the last day of steam on BR in August 1968.

ABOVE: Newly restored LMS 'Black Five' 4-6-0 No. 4767 at the Rail 150 exhibition at Shildon, on August 25, 1975, where it was named *George Stephenson*.

No. 4767 'George Stephenson'

NO. 4767 WAS completed on the last day of the LMS, December 31, 1947 at Crewe works. It was unique among the 842-strong class in that it featured outside Stephenson link motion in addition to other experimental features; a double chimney, Timken roller bearings throughout and electric lighting.

The fitting of outside Stephenson valve gear, for the first time since a GWR Dean Single in 1894, was the result of a chance conversation between HG Ivatt and his opposite number on the GWR, as the GWR Hall 4-6-0s with inside Stephenson motion appeared to outperform the almost identical 'Black Fives' with outside Walschaerts gear. In BR days, No. 44767 worked from Bank Hall up to March 1962, but its double chimney was removed in 1953. After a couple of years at Southport, the engine moved to Kingmoor in November 1964, from where it was withdrawn in December 1967 after a working life of only 20 years.

The engine was sold for scrap to Buttigiegs of Newport but was to be scrapped at Kingmoor. It was purchased by Brian Hollingsworth with the encouragement of Dr Peter Beet, however, the tender was scrapped.

It moved to Steamtown Carnforth in early 1969 but restoration work was slow. On August 14, 1974, it arrived at Thornaby, where volunteers of the North Eastern Locomotive Preservation Group had undertaken to return it to steam within 12 months as it was felt that it was the best choice of 'Black Five' to attend the 150th anniversary of the Stockton and Darlington Railway in at Shildon in 1975. At this time, the owner unexpectedly agreed to sell the locomotive to NELPG's then chairman, Ian Storey.

At Shildon, the former secretary of state for Northern Ireland, William Whitelaw, named No. 4767 after famous railway engineer George Stephenson, whose valve gear the engine carried.

No. 4767 moved immediately to the North Yorkshire Moors Railway, and the first of many main line runs was NELPG's 'Scarborough Flyer' on July 4, 1976 that the 'Black Five' hauled between Newcastle and Stockton. This was followed by regular use on the main line, especially in Scotland, in between NYMR duties.

A particularly well-travelled engine, there are few heritage lines that *George Stephenson* has not visited. It was retubed by NELPG members at Grosmont in 1980, followed by general overhauls at its owner's works at Hepscott, Northumberland, in 1989-1991 when it reappeared in BR black as No. 44767, in 2003-2009.

Nominally now based on the North Norfolk Railway, No. 44767 has not seen main line use in recent years but in November 2014, moved to Butterley for work to prepare it for main line service to be carried out by the Princess Royal Class Locomotive Trust.

No. 44871 'Sovereign'

BUILT AT Crewe in 1945, No. 4871 was allocated to Longsight at Nationalisation when it became No. 44871. It worked from Upperby, Crewe North and Holyhead, then settled at Stoke from July 1952 to November 1962, two years at Crewe South aside.

A move to Trafford Park in June 1963 was followed by Stockport Edgeley in November 1965 and Bolton from May to July 1968, before it ended its days at Carnforth at the end of BR steam in August 1968. It was purchased by Dr Peter Beet and John Parkin and, with No. 44781, hauled BR's last steam train, 1T57, the 'Fifteen Guinea special' from Carlisle to Manchester Victoria via the Settle & Carlisle line on August 11, 1968, being hired back to BR for this duty!

After this it was kept in steam for a couple of days for some BBC filming, becoming the last standard gauge BR steam engine to have its fire dropped. It was preserved at Steamtown Carnforth; steaming at early open days.

Once the BR main line steam ban was lifted it became one of the 'Black Fives' certified for running, initially on the Cumbrian Coast line to Sellafield or south to Leeds. New owners Graham Ellis

> *After this it was kept in steam for a couple of days for some BBC filming, becoming the last standard gauge BR steam engine to have its fire dropped.*

and Willie Johnson moved it north of the border, to Bo'ness on July 14, 1990, from where it saw considerable main line action in Scotland, on the West Highland line and between Aberdeen and Inverness, now carrying the name *Sovereign*.

After expiry of its main line certificate, an overhaul commenced at Bo'ness but by 2002, the owners were concerned at the slow pace of the work and moved it to the ELR for overhaul by Dr Beet's Jubilee Locomotive Company, which was just finishing his Jubilee No. 5690 *Leander*. The 'Black Five's chassis arrived at Bury on December 2, 2002.

However, Riley and Son Engineering, based in Buckley Wells shed and already well-known as operators of classmate No. 45407, purchased No. 44871 in September 2006 moving it to Riley's side of Buckley Wells works for restoration to full main line running condition, including fitment of AWS, TPWS and OTMR and air brakes.

It returned to main line service in December 2009, now unnamed, and is kept extremely busy, often doubleheading with No. 45407 on railtours the length and breadth of Britain.

TOP LEFT: LMS 'Black Five' 4-6-0 No. 44871 climbs through Gleneagles with empty stock from Aberdeen to Bo'ness in September 1992.

BOTTOM LEFT: LMS 'Black Five' 4-6-0s Nos. 44871 and 45407 pass Crubenmore on the climb to Drumochter on the Highland Main Line with Steam Dreams' 'Cathedrals Explorer' on May 13, 2014.

No. 44901

BUILT AT Crewe works in October 1945, No. 4901 was the 602nd 'Black Five' of the 842 built, and incorporated a number of improvements to the original 1934 design.

It was allocated to Carlisle (Kingmoor) shed (12A) where it remained for its entire working life until withdrawal from service in August 1965.

It was sold to Woodham's scrapyard at Barry where it remained for the next 23 years. One of the last stragglers to leave the yard, it moved to the planned preservation centre at Cardiff Bute Street in 1988 but moved back to Barry in 1994 for storage in the shed at the Vale of Glamorgan Railway becoming one of the Barry 10.

It was purchased for restoration at Toddington on the Gloucestershire Warwickshire Railway where it was planned it would receive the boiler from a Turkish 8F but the stripped-down remains have been moved to the embryo preservation scheme on the Sharpness docks branch with plans for its future currently unclear.

No. 44932

BUILT IN 1945, No. 44932 was allocated to Blackpool from September 1950 to January 1952, then Accrington until February 1957, and Agecroft to October 1959, but moved to the GC shed at Annesley from January 1960 until December 1965 (apart from a month at Rose Grove in June/July 1965), until it moved via Derby back to Rose Grove in March 1966.

No. 44932 was withdrawn from Rose Grove shed at the end of steam in August 1968 but in fact spent all of 1968 in store at Kingmoor shed at Carlisle never having moved to Rose Grove. It was, however, purchased for preservation by David Davis and moved to Steamtown at Carnforth on January 1969.

Once the BR main line steam ban was lifted it became one of the 'Black Fives' certified for running, initially on the Cumbrian Coast line to Sellafield or south to Leeds. It was sold by its owner to Steamtown and then later to Peter Wood and Tony Parker before moving to the Midland Railway Centre at Butterley in September 1986. Here it was overhauled, again to main line condition, seeing use in the 1990s until Peter Wood died and his share was acquired by West Coast Railways in 2008, prompting a return to Carnforth for overhaul.

It returned to steam in June 2010 and became a hardworking member of West Coast's fleet from that July.

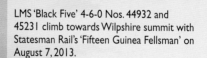

LMS 'Black Five' 4-6-0 Nos. 44932 and 45231 climb towards Wilpshire summit with Statesman Rail's 'Fifteen Guinea Fellsman' on August 7, 2013.

No. 44806 'Magpie'

NO. 4806 WAS built in 1944 and initially allocated to Toton, followed by a number of different Midland Division sheds until it moved to Speke Junction, Merseyside towards the end of steam in June 1967. Its last shed was Lostock Hall from March 30, 1968 until withdrawal right at the end of steam on August 3, 1968, its last BR duty having been as a Preston station pilot.

The engine was saved by David Davis (along with Nos. 44932 and 45407) but was immediately resold to Ken Aldcroft and moved to Steamtown Carnforth on January 7, 1969 to join a growing collection of preserved locomotives. However, the engine moved to Accrington on April 3, 1970 and spent a year at the former L&Y shed where it was the star attraction at the first open day of the East Lancashire Railway, travelling under its own power to Helmshore and back for the August Bank Holiday open weekend.

The ELR did not materialise as planned though and on November 26, 1970, No. 44806 was towed to Haverthwaite, two days before the Lakeside branch connection at Plumpton

ABOVE: LMS 'Black Five' 4-6-0 No. 44806 is seen at Haverthwaite in BR green livery. JEFF COLLEDGE

Junction was lifted. In BR green livery, No. 44806 starred at the opening of the Lakeside & Haverthwaite Railway in 1973 and in May 1974 was named *Magpie* after the children's TV programme. However, in August 1974, a firebox crack was discovered, which could not be repaired at the railway.

And so the engine moved to Steamport at Southport in August 1974 where it was hoped

that repairs could be carried out, but nothing happened and as the site began to wind down, No. 44806 was moved again on August 23, 1983 to the Greater Manchester Museum of Science and Industry at Liverpool Road station, where for the next 10 years it would be a static exhibit.

On February 26, 1993, No. 44806 with its 20-year-old cracked firebox travelled to the Llangollen Railway, where repair work finally began. Its return to steam came on September 15, 1995, and it worked at Llangollen for 10 years, initially as No. 4806 in LMS black livery. A further overhaul then saw the engine back in traffic from September 2007.

Owner Ken Aldcroft died in 2003, the engine passing to his daughter Ms Renee Wyatt, and the engine was named *Kenneth Aldcroft* in recognition of his achievements in preservation, but in July 2013, the locomotive was offered for sale, and was purchased by a supporter of the North Yorkshire Moors Railway who donated it to the NYMR Historical Trust. It moved to the NYMR and took its place in the railway's operating fleet.

ABOVE: LMS 'Black Five' 4-6-0 No. 5000 passes Jubilee No. 5690 *Leander* as it approaches Arley on the Severn Valley Railway on April 12, 1987.

No. 5000

NO. 5000 WAS built at Crewe in 1935 and although numerically the first of its class, it was not the first to be built because Vulcan Foundry had turned out all of its simultaneous but later-numbered order by then. The engine was widely travelled in BR days, working from Rugby until March 1956, when it moved briefly to Carlisle Upperby, then Crewe South in October 1956 to June 1963, apart from short spells at Holyhead. October 1963 saw a move to Chester but withdrawal came in November 1967 after six months at Lostock Hall.

No. 45000 had understandably been selected to represent this extremely successful class as part of the National Collection,

fortunately still carrying a domeless boiler and therefore more is or less 'as-built'. Initially stored at Hellifield after withdrawal, it moved to the store at Preston Park on January 8, 1968 but was placed on loan to the Severn Valley Railway, arriving on November 12, 1977.

It was quickly put back into steam by May 1979, main line certified and in LMS black livery as No. 5000.

It saw 10 years' use and travelled widely, including making an appearance at the Rocket 150 cavalcade at Rainhill in May 1990, but moved to Carnforth in 1990 before becoming a static exhibit at the National Railway Museum.

ABOVE: No. 5000 on Northwich shed on May 18, 1980.

No. 45110 'RAF Biggin Hill'

NO. 5110 WAS built in 1935 by Vulcan Foundry. As No. 45110, it worked from Holyhead for much of its BR career, moving to Stafford in March 1964. It was allocated to Bolton from July 1965 to July 1968, but moved to Lostock Hall for the last few weeks of BR steam. It was one of three members of the class that hauled the 'Fifteen Guinea Special', British Railways' last steam-hauled passenger train, on August 11, 1968. It took the first leg from Liverpool Lime Street to Manchester Victoria at the beginning of the tour before running from Manchester Victoria to Liverpool Lime Street with the returning train at the end of the day's tour. It therefore became the last steam locomotive to haul a BR passenger train and was used in place of sister engine No. 45305, which had been selected for this duty but had been failed with a collapsed brick arch.

After hauling the 'Fifteen Guinea Special', No. 45110 was purchased for preservation and moved to the South Eastern Steam Centre at Ashford, Kent on January 11, 1969, where it was steamed occasionally carrying the name *RAF Biggin Hill*, although it had never carried this in service.

Following the closure of the Ashford centre, it was moved to the Severn Valley Railway on August 18, 1970, where it quickly entered regular service. It has hauled main line steam tours and visited other heritage lines, but its main line certificate had lapsed by 2008 and so it was unable to participate in the 40th anniversary rerun of 1T57. At the end of that day's running on the SVR, No. 45110 returned to Bewdley and its fire was dropped for the last time.

In 2009-10, No. 45110 was placed on static display at Barrow Hill Roundhouse but it returned to Bridgnorth on September 30, 2013 for display in the Engine House at Highley.

ABOVE: LMS 'Black Five' 4-6-0 No. 45110 at Northwood Lane on the SVR on September 11, 1977. The sight of such an authentic train from the BR steam era was extremely rare in preservation at the time.

LEFT: Two stars of the end of BR steam in August 1968, LMS 'Black Five' 4-6-0s Nos. 45110 and 45212 on the 1-in-49 climb from Grosmont to Goathland on the North Yorkshire Moors Railway in August 2008.

No. 45163

NO. 5163 WAS built by Armstrong Whitworth at Newcastle in July 1935 and spent the majority of its working life in Scotland, working from Corkerhill and Perth, before moving to Kingmoor in May 1952, from where it was withdrawn in June 1965. Woodhams purchased it for scrap and it was one of the later departures from Barry, leaving the yard in January 1987 after nearly 22 years there. It was moved to the Humberside Locomotive Preservation Group's base at Dairycoates in Hull where dismantling and restoration commenced.

Early in 1991 the locomotive was offered for sale and negotiations took place to secure the engine for the Colne Valley Railway at Castle Hedingham in Essex. The dismantled locomotive was moved to the CVR in 1993, and once suitable covered accommodation was obtained, restoration work has continued satisfactorily.

No. 45491

NO. 5491 WAS BUILT at Derby in December 1943 and allocated to Corkerhill shed in Glasgow. In July 1952 as BR No. 45491 it was transferred to Kingmoor but was withdrawn in July 1965 and sold to Woodham's scrapyard at Barry. After 16 years it was bought by the West Lancashire Black Five Society and moved first to the ICI works at Hillhouse in 1981 before quickly moving on to the Fleetwood Steam Centre on July 16 that year.

It was purchased by its current owner Phil Wainwright and moved to the Midland Railway Centre at Butterley in September 1991 where restoration continued but it was moved again, to the Great Central Railway in 2011.

Restoration work on the chassis and tender has been virtually completed and work continues mainly on the boiler, with a return to steam expected in the near future.

No. 45293

NO. 5293 WAS completed in December 1936 and allocated initially to Shrewsbury, moving in 1938 to Carnforth followed by various north-western sheds until in April 1942 it settled at Carlisle Upperby for the next 21 years. In 1963 it moved to nearby Kingmoor, from where it was withdrawn in August 1965, and sold to Woodhams at Barry.

The British Rail Enginemen (1A) Steam Preservation Group was formed in July 1980 by a group of locomotive footplatemen from Stonebridge Park depot in North London, to preserve and restore a steam engine, subsequently purchasing a Bulleid Merchant Navy Pacific, No. 35010 *Blue Star* from Barry scrapyard.

The group bought a second locomotive,

'Black Five' No. 45293, on August 26, 1983, but it was to spend a further three years in the yard at Barry (more work parties, grease, oil and paint) while more money was being raised to move it.

Eventually though, on December 11, 1986, No. 45293 was put on to a low loader and moved to a museum site at North Woolwich. Unfortunately as it became clear that it was likely the museum was to close, the group had no alternative but to relocate its engines.

It was agreed that the Colne Valley Railway in Essex would be their new home and after the Merchant Navy had been moved, the 'Black Five' followed it to Castle Hedingham in 1996, where restoration is progressing.

No. 5025

NO. 5025 WAS one of the first batch of the class built by Vulcan Foundry in 1934, and is now the oldest-surviving 'Black Five'. It worked from Perth over the Highland line during its first year in service, but in later BR days worked south of the border, from Upperby between June 1958 and June 1963. After three years at Lancaster, it moved to Carnforth in April 1966 and became one of the last working 'Black Fives', withdrawn at the end of BR steam in August 1968.

However, it was not one that made its preservation home at Carnforth; and having once been a Highland line engine, was purchased by Scottish railway heritage pioneer, Ted Watkinson, for the proposed preserved railway between Aviemore and Grantown-on-Spey, which would become known as the Strathspey Railway.

Ted felt that another preserved railway should have use of the engine until the Strathspey Railway was ready to use it. It moved to Hunslet's works in Leeds for repairs and a repaint into LMS livery on April 25, 1969 and arrived on the Keighley & Worth Valley Railway on June 30, 1969 where it went into service. No. 5025 moved north, firstly for overhaul at Andrew Barclay's works

in Kilmarnock on May 29, 1975 and entered service on the Strathspey Railway between Aviemore and Boat of Garten on August 27, 1975.

1981 saw the engine out on the main line working from Perth over what was once its home turf and it is credited with returning steam to the scenic branch to Kyle of Lochalsh in May 1982. It was withdrawn in 1994 requiring major overhaul with the WEC Watkinson Trust working hard to raise the necessary £354,000. Much of this has been raised and work is in progress so it is hoped No. 5025 should see a return to service in 2016.

BELOW: LMS 'Black Five' No. 45231 climbs past Blea Moor with Statesman Rail's 'Fellsman' from Lancaster to Carlisle via Blackburn on June 10, 2015.

LEFT: LMS 'Black Five' 4-6-0 No. 45212 passes Oakworth on the KWVR with a breakdown train.

No. 45212

NO. 5212 WAS built by Armstrong Whitworth in Newcastle in 1935 and originally allocated to Bradford. It worked from Fleetwood between September 1950 and September 1964, followed by six months at Carnforth, three months at Speke Junction and Kingmoor from September 1965 to January 1968, before ending its days at Lostock Hall shed.

It was withdrawn at the end of BR steam in August 1968, having the distinction of heading BR's penultimate steam-hauled revenue-earning service, the 8.50pm Preston to Blackpool on August 3, 1968. In fact later that night it also shunted sleeping cars at Preston station, complete with passengers, so, arguably qualifying as BR's last-ever scheduled steam passenger working.

In the last week of BR steam, Dr Peter Beet and his colleagues at Carnforth arranged the purchase of Nos. 44806, 45212 and 45231 as well as BR Standard 4MT 4-6-0 No. 75027.

No. 45212 was bought by the Keighley & Worth Valley Railway and arrived on the line in October 1968. The engine was much bigger than anything normally seen on the branch but proved very capable and provided what was, at the time, the unusual sight of a 'Black Five' working passenger trains.

It was a regular KWVR locomotive for very many years but never travelled elsewhere until 1999 from when it was based at the North Yorkshire Moors Railway, where it had been overhauled in a deal sponsored by Peter Best, chairman of the NYMR, under which it ran from late 2002 still making occasional return visits to the KWVR.

In a unique agreement between the KWVR and the Bury-based engineering company Riley & Son (E) Ltd. No. 45212 is now undergoing a major overhaul, which will allow it to operate on the main line while spending three months per year on the KWVR and also visiting other heritage lines.

No. 45231 *'The Sherwood Forester'*

NO. 5231 WAS BUILT by Armstrong Whitworth in 1936 and spent most of its early life at Patricroft shed. It was transferred to Aston, Birmingham in 1954 where it remained for nine years, before moving on via Rugby to Chester in June 1963 where it stayed until closure of the shed in April 1967. One of the 'Black Fives' destined to survive to the end of steam, it moved to Speke Junction and finally Carnforth in May 1968.

It was sold by BR directly to Michael Stephenson for preservation and was restored at Carnforth to LMS black livery, moving to the Great Central Railway in 1973 where it hauled the railway's official opening train between Loughborough and Quorn. In May 1976 it was named *3rd (Volunteer) Battalion The Worcestershire and Sherwood Foresters Regiment* at Quorn, remaining a regular performer on the line.

It moved to the Nene Valley Railway on April 28, 1989 where again it saw regular use but returned to Loughborough on March 24, 1993. It was sold to the GCR in late 1996. Repainted in BR black in 1997, it acquired the simplified name *The Sherwood Forester*.

It was agreed that it would be overhauled at the GCR for main line service after 2002 by Bert Hitchen but in the event, Bert purchased it outright in the December and it returned to steam in 2004. After GCR service, it moved by road to the Mid Hants Railway on February 3, 2005. After a three-month delay over certification issues, it finally entered main line service with a Steam Dreams' 'Cathedrals Express' to Canterbury on June 29, 2005. It had not run on the main line for 37 years since August 1968, but has now become one of the most active and widely travelled of all the preserved class members. Following the owner's death the engine was sold in late 2015, to become a member of Jeremy Hosking's fleet.

ABOVE: Before the second track was lifted, LMS 'Black Five' 4-6-0 No. 5231 accelerates away from Loughborough on the Great Central Railway on June 20, 1976.

ABOVE: In dirty BR black livery, LMS 'Black Five' 4-6-0 No. 45231 heads a photo charter goods train away from Quorn & Woodhouse on the GCR on June 7, 1993.

ABOVE: On its first run after restoration, LMS 'Black Five' 4-6-0 No. 5305 returns from Scarborough on April 30, 1977.

ABOVE: No. 45305 passes GCR O4 2-8-0 No. 63601 as it departs from Loughborough on the GCR.

No. 5305 'Alderman AE Draper'

NO. 5305 WAS built by Armstrong Whitworth of Newcastle in 1936, and spent most of its life based in north-west England, working in BR days from Edge Hill, Crewe South, Willesden, Workington, Chester, Springs Branch and Speke Junction until finding its way to Lostock Hall in May 1968. It survived to the end of steam on BR and was rostered for BR's last steam train, the 'Fifteen Guinea Special' on August 11, 1968 but sadly the night before the trip, was failed with a collapsed brick arch and had to be replaced by sister engine No. 45110.

Withdrawn from Lostock Hall, No. 45305 was sold to scrap merchants Albert Draper and Sons of Hull, who broke up 742 former BR locomotives. No. 45305 should have been the 743rd but was kept until last largely because it was still the cleanest engine in the yard. It was then decided to restore it to working order rather than scrap it.

Albert Draper was, at the time, the president of Hull Kingston Rovers Rugby League FC, and he dreamed that No. 5305 would one day head a special train from Hull to Wembley, where he hoped his club would be playing in the Rugby League Challenge Cup Final.

The Humberside Locomotive Preservation Group was set up to restore the engine and it was based at the former Hull Dairycoates shed. In immaculate LMS black livery, it returned to steam in 1976, heading its first main line railtour, from Leeds via Harrogate to York and Scarborough on April 30 that year.

In 1984, No. 5305 was named *Alderman AE Draper* by the Mayor

of Hedon, Bill Tong. AE Draper was twice Mayor of Hedon. Based at Hull and regularly used in main line service, the locomotive ran until its boiler certificate expired in 1994. The Dairycoates site was eventually sold for redevelopment and the by then large collection of stock, including the locomotive was relocated to a private non-rail connected site at RAF Binbrook in Lincolnshire on November 10, 1995.

However, No. 5305 moved again, arriving on the GCR on November 20, 1996 where it had a much brighter future and was returned to service in August 2003, the 35th anniversary of the end of BR steam, in BR livery as No. 45305. The locomotive remains in the ownership of AE Draper and Sons but in the long-term care of the 5305 Locomotive Association, the successor to the Humberside Locomotive Preservation Group.

Although now permanently based on the GCR, the main line still beckoned and on May 28, 2005, No. 45305 made its first main line trip for 15 years, running from Birmingham to Didcot. It has alternated between the GCR and the main line, but also spent long periods on the KWVR, which is a more convenient base for railtour operations in the north of England.

In 2013, the engine worked the Liverpool to Longsight leg of the Railway Touring Company's 'Fifteen Guinea Special' to celebrate the 45th anniversary of the end of BR steam in 1968.

LEFT: LMS 'Black Five' 4-6-0 No. 45337 climbs the 1-in-49 gradient past Water Ark on the NYMR.

No. 45337

NO. 5337 WAS first allocated to Blackpool, and after moving around various sheds, settled at Agecroft, Manchester (26B) from 1947 to August 1963. After 15 months at Southport, it moved to Kingmoor in November 1964, from where it was withdrawn in February 1965, and sold to Woodham's scrapyard at Barry.

Purchased by the 26B Locomotive Company and moved to the East Lancashire Railway in May 1984, it returned to steam in May 1995, becoming the first ex-Barry 'Black Five' to return to service, and carrying the identity M5337 in early BR livery.

Although used on the ELR for a while, it has spent much of its life in preservation either at Llangollen or the North Norfolk Railway, occasionally visiting other lines. It is regularly renumbered and often runs as well-known named class member, No. 45156 *Ayrshire Yeomanry*.

BELOW: In freezing conditions, LMS 'Black Five' 4-6-0 No. 5305 climbs away from Glenfinnan viaduct on the West Highland extension on December 5, 1989 with a crew-training special.

ABOVE: LMS 'Black Five' 4-6-0 No. 45379 climbs away from Leekbrook Junction on the Churnet Valley Railway towards Cauldon Lowe.

No. 45379

NO. 5379 WAS built by Armstrong Whitworth and entered service in July 1937, allocated to Crewe. It moved to Rugby in 1948 at Nationalisation, but went back to Crewe North in 1956 and then on to Bletchley in 1961. Finally No. 45379 moved to Willesden in 1964 from where it was withdrawn in the summer of 1965, going to Barry scrapyard later that year.

It was bought for restoration and moved to the then Bristol Suburban Railway at Bitton on May 18, 1974. Later though it was moved again, to the Great Central Railway (Nottingham) at Ruddington, where restoration continued slowly. It was resold to the Mid Hants Railway and moved to Alresford on March 1, 2002.

The restoration of No. 45379 took a further five years but was completed in September 2007 when it hauled its first revenue-earning service for more than 45 years, the second Barry 'Black Five' to return to steam.

As well as being a regular member of the MHR operating fleet, the 'Black Five' is well travelled and frequently visits other heritage lines, often in rather more traditional 'Black Five' territory.

ABOVE: LMS 'Black Five' 4-6-0 No. 45379 stripped down for overhaul at Bitton on the Bristol Suburban Railway on July 7, 1985.

ABOVE No. 5379 on arrival at Ropley on the Mid Hants Railway in 2002.
CEDRIC JOHNS

No. 45407 'The Lancashire Fusilier'

NO. 5407 WAS BUILT by Armstrong Whitworth in 1937, the first of a batch of 226 engines, which was the largest order ever placed with a private builder by a British railway company.

It was first allocated to Kettering where it worked on the Midland main line and also worked from Millhouses, Kentish Town and Burton, but in March 1965 moved to Speke Junction, ending up at Lostock Hall in May 1968.

It lasted right to the end of steam in August 1968 and was one of several 'Black Fives' to be preserved at Steamtown Carnforth, having been purchased by David Davis for £3300. It was returned to steam in Furness Railway brown livery but when it returned to the main line in 1973 it was in BR black.

In 1974 it was bought by Paddy Smith who continued to operate the engine on the BR system, mainly in the north-west and north Wales, now in LMS black livery as No. 5407. In May 1984, it was the engine that brought steam back to the West Highland extension from Fort William to Mallaig, where it spent three seasons in the late 1980s. After its last season in Scotland in 1993, No. 5407 was moved to Carnforth for new tyres and on to the East Lancashire Railway for running on heritage lines for the last three years of its boiler ticket.

In 1997 it gained a third private owner when Ian Riley bought it from Paddy Smith and had the engine overhauled at his works in Bury, including the fitting of air brake equipment. Riley had cut his teeth in the steam preservation business assisting Derek Foster with the overhauls of his two ex-Barry engines, LMS 'Jinty' 0-6-0T No. 7298 and BR Standard 2-6-0 No. 76079 at Foster's works at Kirby.

He had formed his own company, Ian Riley Engineering in 1989, but when his father's firm closed, Ian was able to acquire the trading name Riley & Sons (Engineering). In August 1993, the company took a lease on a large part of the ELR's Buckley Wells shed, where the steam overhaul business steadily expanded.

In Riley's ownership, after its return to steam in 1997, No. 45407 has become one of the most well-travelled and consistently reliable engines on the main line, while still seeing regular use on the ELR and the North Yorkshire Moors Railway as well as hardly ever missing a season at Fort William.

After a period running as No. 45157 *The Glasgow Highlander,* it reverted to its correct number but carrying the name *The Lancashire Fusilier,* a regiment once based in Bury.

BELOW: LMS 'Black Five' 4-6-0 No. 45407 running as No. 44996 climbs towards Corrour summit on the West Highland main line.

LEFT: LMS 'Black Five' 4-6-0 No. 5407 departs from Bangor with a 'North Wales Coast Express' on September 9, 1990.

BELOW: 4-6-0 No. 45407 passes Attadale on the Kyle line with the Railway Touring Company's 'North Briton' on April 14, 2008.

LEFT: In LMS livery, LMS 'Black Five' 4-6-0 No. 5407 climbs away from Blackburn past Lower Darwen on the Bolton line on March 24 1989.

No. 45428 '*Eric Treacy*'

NO. 45428 WAS withdrawn from Holbeck shed on September 30, 1967 but was purchased for preservation by Brian Hollingsworth, initially remaining at Holbeck. It was moved to the Standard Gauge Steam Trust at Tyseley, Birmingham on August 24, 1968, where it was restored to LMS livery and named *Eric Treacy*

after the one-time Bishop of Wakefield and well-known steam enthusiast and photographer. It took part in occasional open days at Tyseley, even travelling further afield, though unfortunately not at the head of main line passenger trains.

A more active future beckoned when No. 5428 was moved to the NYMR on November 3-5 1974

where it was quickly put to work on the newly reopened railway, but withdrawn in 1975. It saw further service during the 1980s and in 2001 it was sold to the NYMR for an undisclosed sum. It has remained a regular performer on the line since, now certified for running on the Esk Valley line to Whitby and Battersby.

LMS 'Black Five' 4-6-0 No. 45428 emerges from Grosmont tunnel on the NYMR and passes LNER K1 2-6-0 No. 62005 on April 29,1984.

8F 2-8-0

THE LMS 7F 2-8-0 was very much a heavy freight version of Stanier's 'Black Five' 4-6-0 but has a much more complicated history, seeing extensive service overseas during and after the Second World War. The LMS certainly needed better freight power at the time, relying largely on Midland 4F 0-6-0s and various ancient 0-8-0s, especially of LNWR origin. They were reclassified to the more familiar 8F only after Nationalisation.

The design was chosen to be the country's standard freight design for wartime service, and while the LMS was building them for itself, the War Department ordered 208 from Beyer Peacock and North British as well as requisitioning 51 more.

Stanier 2-8-0 production continued for the WD until 1943, when Riddles' 'Austerity' 2-8-0 became available and were cheaper in view of their more basic design, but the LMS continued to build its engines until 1946.

However, many WD ones found themselves surplus as they were not required in France as originally intended and many were loaned to other British railway companies in 1940-42, carrying temporary LMS numbers. By late 1941, though, they were in demand and most of the WD's Stanier 2-8-0s saw wartime military service overseas in Egypt, Palestine, Iran and Italy, and many were later sold to the local railways in these and other countries such as Turkey and Iraq.

The last 24 new WD ones remained in the UK on loan to the LMS and a total of 31 were sold by the WD to the LMS in 1943. In 1952 five WD ones returned to the UK in poor condition, but were overhauled to work on the Longmoor Military Railway and three were later sold to BR in 1957.

In total, 852 were built between 1935 and 1946, 331 for the LMS between 1935 and 1945. Another 245 were built by the LNER, GWR and SR in 1943-45 nominally for the LMS, but mostly retained on loan for the duration. The LNER purchased another 68 in 1944-46, but sold them to the LMS after the war.

So BR inherited a total of 624 of the class in 1948, purchased 39 more in that year and the last three in 1957. Under BR's power classification system, they became 8Fs. They were spread across the former LMS system, some at LMS sheds on other regions but were always rare north of the border. They were reclassified 8F by BR.

All 666 survived until 1960 and withdrawals did not start in earnest until 1964. The only Scottish Region ones were Nos. 48773–48775, the former LMR ones, and were withdrawn as early as 1962 but were reinstated into LMR stock in 1963. No less than 150 survived to 1968, the last year of steam on BR, and one of those that lasted right to the end was former Longmoor and Scottish Region No. 48773, which was the only one purchased from BR for preservation.

More were preserved after periods at Barry scrapyard, several have returned to steam but at least one looks likely to disappear, while several are preserved in other countries and several Turkish ones have been repatriated to Britain, one even being re-exported for preservation in Israel. in the UK.

No. 48151

NO. 8151 WAS built in 1942 at Crewe and after a year at Kingmoor, was allocated to Grangemouth until 1949 when it was transferred to Wellingborough for six years. Next came a move to Canklow (19C) near Sheffield from 1955 to 1963, and Barrow Hill (now the Roundhouse). It also saw service from Edge Hill in Liverpool and finally Northwich up to withdrawal in January 1968.

It was sold to Woodhams at Barry but bought for preservation, arriving at Embsay on December 1, 1975 but restoration made little progress until it was resold to David Smith and moved to the Procor wagon works at Horbury Junction in 1982. A further move to Butterley took place in 1987 and the engine returned to steam in June that year.

Its first railtour was on October 24, 1987 from Derby to Buxton, actually as a last-minute substitute for *Flying Scotsman*, and the engine found itself a popular main line performer, being one of a select number with balanced driving wheels and more suited to passenger service.

It moved to Carnforth on July 23, 1990, where David Smith was to establish West Coast Railways as a Train Operating Company over the coming years, and the 8F has always taken a prominent part in operations, being seen in all parts of the country, as far north even as Wick and Thurso.

In 2014, No. 48151 made its first operational visit to a heritage railway, visiting the Mid Norfolk Railway at Dereham for its West Coast steam gala, trebleheading the empty stock from Carnforth with Jubilee No. 45699 *Galatea* and Royal Scot No. 46115 *Scots Guardsman*.

LMS 8F 2-8-0 No. 48151 emerges from Dove Holes tunnel on the MR main line to Manchester on October 24, 1987.

ABOVE: LMS 8F 2-8-0 No. 48151 crosses Invershin viaduct on the Far North line with the Railway Touring Company's 'Great Britain' railtour in April 2007.

ABOVE: LMS 8F 2-8-0 No. 48151 at Embsay on June 19, 1976

ABOVE: No. 48151 heads a ballast train on the Settle & Carlisle line at Horton-in-Ribblesdale in December 2000. BRIAN DEAN

RIGHT: LMS 8F 2-8-0 No. 48151 departs from Skipton with a Carnforth – Scarborough train on September 25, 1993.

ABOVE: LMS 8F 2-8-0 No. 48151, Jubilee 4-6-0 No. 45699 *Galatea* and Royal Scot 4-6-0 No. 46115 *Scots Guardsman* climb Giggleswick bank with empty stock from Dereham to Carnforth in May 2014.

No. 48305

NO. 8305 WAS completed at Crewe in November 1943, and by early BR days was working from Wellingborough shed. In April 1957, it was transferred to Northampton until moving to Crewe South in December 1962 until July 1965. It spent three months at Northwich and ended its days at to Speke Junction from where it was withdrawn in January 1968. It arrived at Woodhams in September 1968.

No. 48305 was bought for preservation by Roger Hibberd and arrived on the GCR on November 20, 1985. The long job of restoration to working order at Loughborough, including building a new tender, took 10 years and it entered traffic on February 25 1995.

As well as the GCR, No. 48305 spent some time at the Midland Railway – Butterley, North Norfolk and Gloucestershire and Warwickshire railways. It made an appearance at the GCR(N) at Ruddington in 2000 and worked the line's first passenger train to Rushcliffe Halt on June 10 that year, and then worked for five years on the Churnet Valley Railway, after which it was moved to L&NWR at Crewe for a 10-year overhaul.

Money was made available from The David Clarke Railway Trust for the boiler repairs and No. 48305 returned to the GCR on April 13, 2006, returning to traffic in May, but the engine was withdrawn for another 10-year overhaul towards the end of 2011, which remains in progress.

ABOVE: LMS 8F 2-8-0 No. 48305 heads coal empties past Kinchley Lane on the GCR on February 25, 1995.

No. 48518

NO. 8518 WAS unique among preserved 8Fs in having been one of 30 built by the LNER at Doncaster in 1944 and worked as an LNER class O6 until the end of the war when it was taken into LMS stock, working out of Swansea on the Central Wales line to Shrewsbury. It was later allocated to Willesden followed by a few months at Croes Newydd in 1964-65.

It was withdrawn in 1965 and sent to Barry scrapyard from where it was one of the very last departures in February 1988, as part of what became known as the 'Barry 10'.

This motley collection of assorted utterly derelict engines, which nobody wanted, was purchased by the South Glamorgan Council and moved to a proposed steam centre at Bute Street station in Cardiff but when nothing came of this, they were all moved back to Barry in 1994. Here they were put under cover in the old steam shed at what was then the Vale of Glamorgan Railway.

They could not be disposed of as the council had ceased to exist and ownership was extremely unclear but in 2003 a deal was announced that would see the engines released and gradually the engines were disposed of, but they tend to still be the forgotten engines of preservation. No. 48518 was acquired in order that its boiler could donate its firebox to the new boiler being built for a GWR County 4-6-0 at Didcot.

The engine was moved to Llangollen for the boiler to be removed, with other parts being used by the new-build LMS Patriot project. Only the wheels and frames will survive intact and the engine must to all intents and purposes now be regarded as scrapped.

LEFT:
No. 48518 in store on the Vale of Glamorgan Railway at Barry.
ROBIN JONES

No. 48173

NO. 8173 EMERGED from Crewe works in June 1943 and entered service at Willesden but in February 1948 was reallocated to Newton Heath and in December 1949 transferred to Rugby where it stayed until January 1965 when it moved briefly to Mold Junction from where it was withdrawn in July that year.

No. 48173 moved to Woodhams at Barry, from where it was purchased by a group of Avon Valley Railway members, the 8F Preservation Group and moved to the AVR, the 200th locomotive to leave the yard, arriving at Bitton on September 10, 1988.

The engine was resold to a director of the Churnet Valley Railway, arriving at Cheddleton in December 2007, where it remains in store in very poor condition awaiting overhaul.

ABOVE: Maroon-liveried No. 48624 heads a coal train on the Great Central Railway in October 2014.

No. 48624

INTERESTINGLY, representatives of 8Fs built by all the Big Four companies survived at Barry and No. 8624 was the Southern-built one, completed in 1943 at Ashford. Unusually it spent its entire working life allocated to Willesden.

It was withdrawn in 1965 and not rescued from the scrapyard until July 1981 when it was moved to Peak Rail's site at Buxton. The decision by Peak Rail to relocate from Buxton to Darley Dale, saw No. 48624 move there in 1991.

It took no less than 28 years of hard work, mostly in the open air, before the locomotive returned to traffic in May 2009 at Peak Rail, unexpectedly carrying LMS maroon livery as No. 8624. Unfortunately Peak Rail was unable to offer the locomotive the amount of revenue-earning work it needed and it was moved to the GCR in March 2011, where it has regained its BR identity but remained in maroon livery.

It had taken part in the reopening weekend of the Cauldon Lowe branch from the Churnet Valley Railway in November 2010, and has also worked on the Mid-Norfolk Railway. 2014 saw the engine repainted into authentic BR black livery.

ABOVE: No. 48624 under restoration at Darley Dale on Peak Rail. ROBIN JONES

No. 8233

THIS 8F IS THE only one to have been purchased straight out of BR service and has a unique history, having been built in 1940 by North British for War Department service in France. However, the occupation of France saw WD No. 307 working on the LMS instead as No. 8233, from Toton, Holbeck and Westhouses sheds.

But by December 1941, the WD wanted it back to send it to Persia. It ran as Iranian State Railways No. 41.109 and was used for supply trains to the Russian army. In 1946 the engine was transferred overland to the Suez Canal Zone, now becoming WD No. 70307, on loan for two years to Egyptian State Railways. Needing a new firebox, it came close to being scrapped in 1948 but eventually found its way back to Derby works in 1952, where repairs were completed in 1954.

It stayed in the UK but still in WD service,

working on the Longmoor Military Railway, now as WD No. 500.

In 1957, the engine's National Service ended and, along with two other Longmoor 8Fs, it finally joined BR's other 665 8Fs as No. 48773, at Polmadie shed in Glasgow. The Scottish Region only had these three 8Fs and withdrew them fairly quickly, but the London Midland Region still had use for them and they were reinstated. Late in 1963, No. 48773 moved to Carlisle Kingmoor, then Stockport Edgeley, Buxton, Bolton in September 1964, and finally Rose Grove in July 1968, where it not only lasted right to the end of BR steam but saw use on farewell to steam railtours, and participated in the grand finale of steam over Copy Pit summit.

With only 36000 miles on the clock after a heavy intermediate repair at Crewe in 1966, No. 48773 was an ideal candidate for preservation. The 8F Society was late

in starting its appeal but it was successful and bought the engine from BR, moving it first to Tyseley, then to the Severn Valley Railway where it arrived on January 4, 1969 in working order.

Few locomotives have managed to work on six railways in three continents, carrying six different identities and escaping the scrap merchants at least six times in the process, and its remarkable story certainly did not end there. It was a regular and popular engine on the SVR for many years and in 1975, it ran under its own steam to Shildon to participate in the Rail 150 cavalcade.

Following this, with main line certification it became a popular main line performer, having the honour of heading the first singleheaded steam train in preservation up the Lickey incline on January 2, 1999. Needing another major overhaul, it is on display in the Engine House at Highley.

No. 8431

NO. 8431 IS unique among the preserved 8Fs in having been built by the GWR at Swindon and entered service on the GWR during the war, working from Newton Abbott, then Gloucester until March 1947, only becoming an LMS engine on cessation of hostilities and moving to Royston in West Yorkshire until August 1955. However, it then returned to the Western Region, spending five years at Bristol St Phillips Marsh, two years at Old Oak Common, and two years at Barrow Road before withdrawal from Bath Green Park in 1964, and sale to Woodhams in Barry.

It was purchased by the KWVR and arrived by road at Haworth in May 1972. As an early departure from the scrapyard it was restored remarkably quickly, steam-tested by the end of 1974 and entered service in December 1975.

It remained in regular use but has made few visits away from home apart from visiting the GWS at Didcot in 1985 in GWR livery. It is now on static display at Oxenhope.

ABOVE: 8F No. 8431 at Didcot carrying GWR livery in May 1985.

LEFT: No. 48773 became the first steam locomotive in the preservation era to tackle the Lickey bank with a passenger train, on January 2, 1999. COLOUR-RAIL.COM

TCDD No. 45160

THIS ENGINE was built in 1940 as WD 348 by North British for use on the Western Front, but with the fall of France, it found itself working instead as LMS No. 8274 for a few weeks before being shipped to Turkey as a kit of parts with 19 others. It worked for the Turkish Railways (TCDD) as No. 45160 into the 1980s.

It was the first of the Turkish 8Fs to be repatriated by the Churchill 8F Company, arriving at Swanage in June 1989 where it was restored to operational condition at nearby Hamworthy.

It moved for a while to the ELR but then to the Gloucestershire Warwickshire Railway, where it was based for several years after it returned to steam in April 2010. In 2014 though, it moved to Ruddington for regular service on the Great Central Railway (Nottingham).

ABOVE: Restored TCDD 8F 2-8-0 No. 45160 and newly repatriated No. 45166 at the Barry Island Railway in 2011. MICHAEL WILCOCK

TCDD No. 45166

MANY YEARS after the successful repatriation of No. 45160, the Churchill 8F Company decided to save two more of the Turkish 8Fs, the engines chosen being No. 45166 and 45170 (WD 341 and 554).

In a huge logistical exercise, Andrew Goodman of Moveright International managed to move both engines across Turkey from Sivas in 2010, the story being the subject of a Monster Moves documentary.

Both engines spent some time at Barry Island, and variously visited Locomotion and the North Norfolk Railway until in the absence of any other offers to purchase and restore it, No. 45166 was sold to the Municipality of Beersheba, Israel in December 2012.

It is currently displayed at the former Be'er Sheva Turkish railway station on the former railway to Beersheba as Israel Railways No. 70414, which was believed to be the last steam engine to run in Israel.

ABOVE: No. 45166 at the former Be'er Sheva station as Israel Railways No. 70414.
CHEN MELLING.

TCDD No. 45170

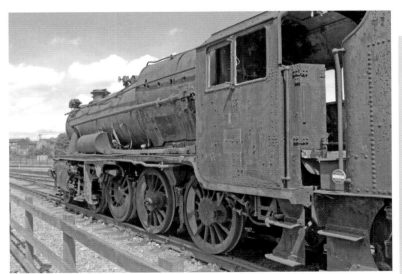

ABOVE: Turkish 8F 2-8-0 No. 45170 at the Locomotion museum at Shildon.

WD 554 was also recovered from Sivas in December 2010 by the Churchill 8F Trust and found its way to Ian Storey's works at Hepscott, Northumberland where offers were invited for its purchase. In late 2014, it was sold to the Scottish Railway Preservation Society and moved to Bo'ness for restoration and possibly even main line use.

No. 1429

ABOVE: Iraqi Railways No. 1429 derelict near Baghdad. DEREK BIRD

Jubilee 4-6-0

STANIER'S 5XP express 4-6-0 was to become the 191-strong Jubilee class, painted maroon and known initially as 'Red Fives'. Sir Henry Fowler's parallel-boilered Patriot 4-6-0s were still being built, but the last five were built with Stanier's taper boiler and so became the first of the Jubilees.

Introduced in a bit of a hurry along with the 'Black Five' 4-6-0s with 113 Jubilees going straight into service, they were not a great success and comments from footplate crews included the classic, "the black 'uns are alright but the red 'uns won't steam". A moderate degree of superheating was partly to blame but changes to the blastpipe and chimney dimensions helped to transform them.

On April 29, 1935 No. 5552, the first of the class, permanently swapped identities with No. 5642, which had been named *Silver Jubilee* 10 days earlier in recognition of the silver jubilee of King George V on May 6. It was this decision to swap identities with No. 5552, which meant that *Silver Jubilee* became the first engine,

carrying unlined black livery with chrome embellishments, and thus gave its name to the class.

A consistent naming theme was impossible for such a large class, so once Commonwealth countries and states were exhausted, there was a series of admirals and naval commanders and then British Navy warships, mostly originally characters in Greek mythology but with quite a mixture of various themes towards the end.

They are often associated with the former MR main line where they represented a big increase in power over the Compound 4P 4-4-0s. Right up until the late 1950s, it was still rare for anything bigger than a Jubilee to work south of Leeds. With so many engines, the class could nevertheless be found on main lines throughout the former LMS system.

There were a number of detail differences, the most obvious being that some entered service with Fowler tenders. In January 1951, the power classification was changed from 5XP to 6P by BR and to 6P5F in November 1955.

Two had been rebuilt in July 1943, being reclassified 6P by the LMS and 7P under BR in 1951. These engines were closer to the rebuilt Royal Scot design than the Jubilee. Another engine, No. 45596 *Bahamas* was fitted with a double chimney by BR.

No. 45637 *Windward Islands* was scrapped in 1952 after the Harrow & Wealdstone crash but although normal withdrawals started in 1960, the last survivors worked from the Leeds area until the end of September 1967, still having been regularly rostered for Settle & Carlisle line expresses during the summer.

The last Jubilee on the London Midland Region, the double-chimneyed No. 45596 *Bahamas* was purchased for preservation in 1966 as was one of the last three on the Eastern Region at Holbeck in 1967, No. 45593 *Kolhapur*. Two much earlier withdrawals, which worked from Bristol, found their way to Barry scrapyard and were subsequently preserved, all four eventually becoming popular stars of the preservation era, though so far the four have not been seen in steam together.

ABOVE: Briefly carrying postwar LMS black livery, LMS Jubilee 4-6-0 No. 5593 *Kolhapur* passes Woodthorpe Lane on the GCR on June 5, 1994.

BELOW: On the Settle & Carlisle line for the first time in 20 years, LMS Jubilee 4-6-0 No. 5593 *Kolhapur* departs from Appleby on March 21, 1987.

No. 5593 *Kolhapur*

NO. 5593 WAS built in 1934 by North British of Glasgow, and in May 1936, in accordance with the Commonwealth theme of the naming policy for the class, was named *Kolhapur* after a state in western India. *Kolhapur* had the distinction of hauling the train carrying Sir Winston Churchill from Liverpool on his return from the North Atlantic Treaty talks with President Roosevelt in the USA in 1942.

It was a well-travelled engine and spent time at various sheds on the LMR in BR days, including Longsight, then Carlisle Upperby from 1951 to 1960, Willesden, Aston, Burton, Patricroft and Newton Heath, until transferred to Leeds Holbeck in the North Eastern Region on March 23, 1965.

The NER Jubilees were to outlast the LMR members of the class with three surviving at Holbeck until the end of steam in the West Riding on September 30, 1967. No. 45593 was withdrawn along with Nos. 45562 *Alberta* and 45697 *Achilles* which had all still seen use on S&C expresses during the summer.

Kolhapur was bought by the then Standard Gauge Steam Trust and quickly moved to Tyseley on October 10, 1967. Restored to LMS maroon livery, No. 5593 regularly appeared at the extremely popular Tyseley open days, which were the nearest thing to working main line steam during the BR ban. Although it travelled further afield a couple of times it was not at the head of a main line passenger train and although on the 'approved' list when the BR ban was lifted, it required boiler work and remained out of steam for many years.

No. 5593 was overhauled at Tyseley and finally returned to the main line; its inaugural run being at the head of HRH The Duke of Gloucester's Royal Train from Tyseley to Birmingham Moor Street on June 5, 1985. After this, various main line runs took place mainly in the Midlands but including a welcome return to the Settle & Carlisle line in March 1987.

October 12, 1989 though saw a transfer to the Great Central Railway where it worked for several years apart from occasional visits to other heritage lines including the ELR, Nene Valley, Llangollen and the Battlefield line. In 1994 No. 5593 was painted black and briefly carried the identity and livery of class pioneer No. 5552 *Silver Jubilee* for the silver jubilee of the preserved GCR. On the ELR, it ran in BR black livery with a Fowler tender, but was repainted into BR green in 1995.

After a period as a static exhibit at Barrow Hill Roundhouse, *Kolhapur* has returned to Tyseley and will be overhauled once the centre's other original main line star, GWR 4-6-0 No. 7029 *Clun Castle* is completed.

ABOVE: In BR black livery and with a Fowler tender from a 4F 0-6-0, LMS Jubilee 4-6-0 No. 45593 running as No. 45698 *Amethyst* stands at Ramsbottom on the ELR on September 24, 1992.

ABOVE: No. 5593, in the guise of No. 5552 *Silver Jubilee*, at Loughborough on June 5, 1994.

BELOW: LMS Jubilee 4-6-0 No. 45596 *Bahamas* heads a 'North Wales Coast Express' past Abergele on October 10, 1993.

No. 45596 *Bahamas*

NO. 5596 WAS built by North British in Glasgow towards the end of 1934, entering traffic in January 1935, allocated to Crewe. It was named *Bahamas* in June 1936.

It also worked from Preston, Camden, Willesden, Kentish Town and Derby before the war and Grimesthorpe, Millhouses and Bristol during it, before returning to Crewe by 1947. In BR days it was allocated to Huddersfield until 1962 and was unique in being fitted with a double chimney at Crewe in May 1961. This turned out to be the last experiment by BR to improve the performance of its steam locomotives, and although tests suggested a significant improvement in steaming, it had all taken too long and the BR experiments terminated in 1962 without any further Jubilees receiving double chimneys.

No. 45596 was returned to traffic based at Carlisle, but was transferred to Stockport Edgeley in July 1962, from where it was withdrawn in July 1966, by then the last of its class in service on the London Midland Region.

After a successful fundraising campaign, the engine was purchased by the Bahamas Locomotive Society in 1967 and sent to Hunslets in Leeds in September 1967 for overhaul and a repaint into its LMS maroon livery, returning to Edgeley on March 11, 1968.

Edgeley shed was never going to be a permanent base and after its closure towards the end of BR steam in the North West in May 1968, *Bahamas* went into store at Bury shed. However, the society located a suitable permanent base and took a lease on the one-time one-road GCR locomotive shed at Dinting; the junction for Glossop on the Woodhead line. *Bahamas* arrived at Dinting under its own steam on November 15, 1968.

This led to the creation of the Dinting Railway Centre, which grew to be an important centre for main line steam. *Bahamas* was selected for use on main line tours after the lifting of the BR ban in 1972 and worked its first railtour, from Hereford to Shrewsbury on October 14, 1972. However, after a run on the Hope Valley route in June 1973 repairs were needed and *Bahamas* had to wait a very long time for these.

Work on the restoration of other locomotives by society volunteers prevented a start on the overhaul of *Bahamas* until 1980, and it was to be a further eight years before it was completed, at a cost of £16,000.

Restored to authentic BR green livery this time, No. 45596 successfully operated 37 railtours on the main line between 1989 and 1994, covering more than 12,000 miles.

This was followed by visits to various heritage railways until the expiry of its boiler certificate in 1997 resulted in its withdrawal from operation. The Dinting Railway Centre was forced to closed in 1991, and the society and its collection moved to Ingrow West on the KWVR; *Bahamas* arriving there on July 14, 1990.

There followed another long period on static display but in 2012 an application was made to the Heritage Lottery Fund to enable the overhaul of *Bahamas* to be undertaken by contractors. The bid was successful, and in December 2013, work commenced at Tyseley with a return to traffic forecast for 2017.

ABOVE: LMS Jubilee 4-6-0 No. 45596 *Bahamas* accelerates away from Nottingham on June 4, 1989.

ABOVE: No. 5596 *Bahamas* at the Dinting Railway Centre on June 20, 1976.

ABOVE: No. 45596 *Bahamas* departs from Derby on June 4, 1989.

No. 5690 *Leander*

NO. 5690 WAS BUILT at Crewe in March 1936 and named *Leander* after *HMS Leander*, which in turn was named after the Greek hero of that name. Allocated first to Crewe, then Derby and Leeds, by Nationalisation in 1948, *Leander* was based at Bristol Barrow Road, where it stayed until March 1964.

After withdrawal in 1964, *Leander* was sold to Woodham's scrapyard at Barry, from where it was rescued by Brian Oliver in May 1972. It was restored at Derby works and, having returned to steam in LMS maroon livery as No. 5690 in June, was based at Dinting Railway Centre from August 25, 1973.

Its railtour debut was on the Hope Valley route on September 1, 1973, at which point it took over from No. 5596 *Bahamas* as the centre's main line flagship but a move to Steamtown Carnforth took place on February 24, 1979 at the head of a railtour from Guide Bridge via Sheffield, York and Leeds.

A period of regular main line use followed and after a working visit to the SVR from August 1980, the engine was moved to the line permanently in April 1984, becoming its main line flagship.

After later purchase by the railway and continued running on the SVR and the main line, it was sold was sold to Dr Peter Beet, the

original founder of Steamtown, in January 1995, but was restored on the East Lancashire Railway, entering service in early 2003, and inaugurating the Heywood extension on September 6 that year. *Leander* returned to the main line in the summer of 2005, to become a main line favourite once again after a break of more than 20 years.

Sadly Dr Beet died in October of that year and in April 2012, *Leander* was withdrawn for overhaul, now in the care of Peter's son, Chris,

with the overhaul this time being carried out by West Coast Railways at Carnforth.

The engine returned in October 2014 unexpectedly in BR black mixed-traffic black livery as carried by some class members in the early 1950s. *Leander* remains in the ownership of the Beet family, and is operated by West Coast Railways from its Carnforth base, where Chris Beet is a locomotive engineer. A full return to main line service took place in early 2015.

RIGHT: LMS Jubilee 4-6-0 No. 5690 *Leander* crosses the Victoria Bridge over the River Severn near Arley on the SVR on June 12, 1988.

ABOVE: No. 5690 *Leander* passes Conwy Castle with a Vintage Trains' excursion from Tyseley in September 2005.

ABOVE: LMS Jubilee 4-6-0 No. 5690 *Leander* approaches Chinley on February 24, 1979 during its move from Dinting to its new base at Carnforth.

BELOW In BR black livery, No. 45690 *Leander* climbs the 1-in-47 incline of Miles Platting bank out of Manchester Victoria on May 30, 2015 with the Railway Touring Company's 'East Yorkshireman' heading for Scarborough.

No. 45699 *Galatea*

NO. 5699 WAS one of the later Jubilees, built at Crewe in April 1936. Like many of the class it was named after a Royal Navy warship, *HMS Galatea*, which had in turn been named after a character from Greek mythology.

King Pygmalion of Cyprus was turned into a sculptor and fell in love with an ivory statue he created. In answer to his prayers, the Goddess Venus brought the statue to life, but it was nameless. In more recent times, more than one writer gave the statue the name Galatea, which is Greek for "she who is milk-white".

In early BR days, the engine worked from Bristol Barrow Road shed but moved to Shrewsbury in October 1961 from where it was withdrawn in November 1964. Stored briefly at Eastleigh works, it was sold to Woodham's scrapyard in January 1965.

There were two Jubilees at Barry but while one, No. 45690 *Leander* became an early purchase, by a company called Oliver Taylor &

Crossley, with big plans and a budget to match, no-one was interested in poor old No. 45699, with one of its middle driving wheels cut in two.

Once the owners had moved *Leander* to Steamtown at Carnforth in 1979, they decided to purchase what remained of *Galatea* from Barry as a source of spare parts and it duly arrived at Carnforth in April 1980. In reality, there are few spare parts on a derelict Barry hulk, it consisted of little more than frames, cylinders and boiler, but it was thought that the boiler might be of use in due course.

The SVR purchased *Leander* in 1984 along with the remains of *Galatea* but eventually it was sold again, to a group from the railway for restoration. The boiler was reunited with the frames and it was moved to Kidderminster on April 17, 1987.

Although *Galatea* had gone beyond being just regarded as a source of spare parts for

Leander, its restoration made little progress and after moving to Tyseley on April 13, 1995, 15 years after leaving Barry, restoration was still slow.

The SVR sold *Leander* and so *Galatea*'s chance of salvation did not really come until it was purchased by David Smith's West Coast Railway company, moving back to Carnforth on July 12, 2002, to undergo one of the heaviest overhauls carried out on a main line locomotive.

No. 45699 made a test run with five coaches round the Carnforth-Hellifield-Blackburn circuit on April 16, 2013, in unlined maroon but carrying the BR 45699 front numberplate. It entered main line service on May 19 on a private charter from King's Lynn to Ipswich, having hauled the empty stock from Carnforth, in lined-out BR maroon livery, as carried by certain LMS Pacifics after 1957, but never a Jubilee.

LEFT: LMS Jubilee 4-6-0 No. 45699 *Galatea* departs from King's Lynn with a private charter train on May 19, 2013, its first passenger working in preservation.

ABOVE: The derelict remains of No. 45699 at Kidderminster on the SVR.
PAUL BASON

ABOVE: LMS Jubilee 4-6-0 No. 45699 *Galatea*, under restoration at West Coast Railways' base at Carnforth in July 2008.

LMS Jubilee 4-6-0 No. 45699 *Galatea* tops Ais Gill summit on July 30, 2015 with West Coast Railways' 'Dalesman'.

Royal Scot 4-6-0

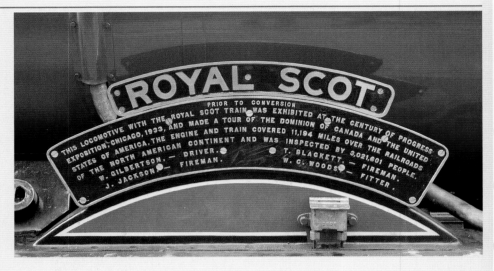

ALTHOUGH INITIALLY the LMS persisted with the small-engine policy inherited from the Midland, Fowler started thinking seriously about a compound Pacific in 1926, however, for various reasons, the LMS management decided to hire four-cylindered 4-6-0 No. 5000 *Launceston Castle* from the GWR, tried it out for a month between Euston and Carlisle and asked Swindon if it could have the drawings.

The GWR declined but in view of its obvious success, the LMS encouraged Fowler to curb his ambitions slightly and think about a three-cylinder simple 4-6-0 and the result was the Royal Scot. These engines were needed urgently and 50 were ordered from North British, which could deliver them within a year. The engines were designed jointly by North British and Derby works partly following a set of drawings from the Southern Railway's four-cylindered Lord Nelson 4-6-0. Although Fowler took little part in the design, it inevitably followed Derby traditions and is recognisable as a typical Fowler engine, with a big parallel boiler, and a disproportionately small tender.

They went straight into service in 1927 on West Coast Main Line expresses and Derby built a further 20. Fortunately they proved successful from the start, although with such an increase in power over their predecessors, this was perhaps inevitable.

They were initially named after British Army regiments or historic LNWR locomotives, although the latter fairly quickly received regimental names.

From late 1931, straight-sided smoke deflectors were added, later replaced by deflectors with angled tops, but their reign on the top expresses was brief as William Stanier replaced them with Pacifics in less than 10 years.

There was also the experimental high-pressure version, numbered 6399 and named *Fury*, which was never entirely satisfactory, and suffered a disastrous boiler failure. It was rebuilt into a conventional locomotive, but remained quite different from the others.

Stanier decided to replace the parallel boilers of the Royal Scots with his taper boiler, and with the replacement of the Fowler tenders with Stanier ones, the 'converted' Royal Scots appear to owe more to Stanier's design thinking than Fowler's. The mechanical dimensions and design though were unchanged.

Conversion started in 1943 but was not completed until 1955. Stanier did not initially fit smoke deflectors but a few received them in the last days of the LMS with BR completing the job. Although primarily WCML engines, once displaced by Stanier Pacifics, the class was used on Settle & Carlisle services, Liverpool to York and some other Midland main line trains including St Pancras-Manchester, but started to be phased out from around 1960, the last one being withdrawn in 1965 from Carlisle Kingmoor.

Fortunately two Royal Scots have survived, including the last one in service, but their stories are sadly similar in that both returned to steam only briefly in the 1970s, then spent much of the next 40 years of their preservation careers as either static exhibits or worse still, stripped down with uncertain futures.

However, their fortunes have both picked up with No. 46115 *Scots Guardsman* finally becoming the main line star it always deserved to be, in 2008, and No. 6100 *Royal Scot* returning to steam briefly the follwing year, and finally expected to make a full-scale return to main line service in February 2016.

BELOW: Heading passenger trains for the first time in preservation, No. 6100 passes Nornvis Bridge on the West Somerset Railway in March 2009. JOHN BOWLER

No. 6100 *Royal Scot*

NO. 6100 WAS the first of the class, built in 1927 by North British in Glasgow and named *Royal Scot,* starting a regimental naming policy for the class.

But in 1933, No. 6100 permanently changed identities with No. 6152 *The King's Dragoon Guardsman*. No. 6152 had been built at Derby in 1930, and this 'new' *Royal Scot* was sent to the Century of Progress Exposition of 1933, touring Canada and the United States with a train of LMS coaches.

In 1950, No. 46100 was fitted with a taper boiler by BR, in accordance with the conversion programme initiated by Stanier, and worked on the WCML from Camden until November 1959, when it moved to Nottingham to work expresses to St Pancras via Melton Mowbray. Following dieselisation of the Midland main line, it became an early withdrawal from service in October 1962.

It was bought by Billy Butlin and, after external restoration at Crewe works to LMS maroon livery, No. 6100 was towed from Crewe to Nottingham on June 12, 1963 by 'Black Five' No. 45038 and then to Boston by B1 4-6-0 No. 61177. After a few days at Boston shed it was taken to Skegness by an Ivatt 4MT mogul No. 6100 and arrived for display at Butlin's holiday camp at Ingoldmells

near Skegness on a Pickfords' low loader on July 18 piped in by the 1st Battalion, The Royal Scots.

A change of policy by Butlin's saw No. 6100 loaned to the Bressingham Steam Museum in Norfolk, where it arrived on March 17, 1971, being quickly returned to steam in 1972. It gave footplate rides at the museum until 1978 and was sold by Butlin's to Bressingham in May 1989.

Plans were eventually made in 2002 for the engine to be overhauled at Bressingham with the aid of an HLF grant of £221,000, to run at the museum in summer and on the main line in winter. The stripped-down engine was moved to Southall in late 2004.

While the overhaul progressed and controversy raged over whether it should carry non-authentic LMS livery, and if so whether it should have smoke deflectors or not, the engine was found to be seriously mechanically flawed, and Bressingham simply did not have the resources to put it right. In a surprise move, it was transferred to Pete Waterman's L&NWR Heritage workshops in Crewe on February 6, 2009, pending a decision on how to proceed.

It was quickly put in steam and made its passenger-hauling debut at the West Somerset Railway's gala weekend in March, but not until

after repairs to the damage caused when the low-loader carrying it to the railway caught fire. The engine also played a starring role in the Steel Steam & Stars II gala at Llangollen in April, but all was not well. This was not to be Royal Scot's finest hour after all.

A sale to Jeremy Hosking's Royal Scot Locomotive and General Trust (RSL&GT) was agreed in July that year, which would see Bressingham reimbursed for the money it had spent, but the sale would not take effect until the engine had received main line certification. It was then discovered that there was a fault with the alignment of Royal Scot's driving axles, which would be very expensive to rectify. The engine was put to one side at Crewe, but the new trust took ownership in March 2010 as this was the only way the engine's overhaul was ever going to be completed.

2015 saw work to rectify the engine's faults being carried out at Crewe and by August it was complete, carrying a coat of green paint. It moved by road to the Severn Valley Railway for running in and entered public service at the September 17-20 steam gala weekend. Following a main line test run on December 22, it is expected to finally enter main line passenger service for the first time in 53 years, on February 6 2016.

LEFT: *Royal Scot's* boiler is lifted off at Bressingham on September 4 2002.

ABOVE: In BR green livery No. 46100 *Royal Scot* crosses Oldbury viaduct on the Severn Valley Railway on October 25, 2105.

ABOVE: Hauling its first train on the main line for 53 years, No. 46100 *Royal Scot* approaches Clapham with a test train from West Coast Railways' Carnforth base on December 22, 2015. DAVE RODGERS

LMS Royal Scot 4-6-0 No. 46115 *Scots Guardsman*
passes Eldroth on a test run from Carnforth to
Hellifield on February 6, 2013.

No. 46115 *Scots Guardsman*

NO. 6115 WAS built by North British in 1927 and named *Scots Guardsman* in 1928 after the Scots Guards. A star of the 1936 film, Night Mail, it was one of the early class members to be fitted with a taper boiler, by the LMS in 1947, and was painted in LMS 1946-style black livery. Being the first of the rebuilt engines to receive smoke deflectors, it became the only one to run with them as an LMS engine. In BR days, No. 46115 worked from Longsight until June 1964 but ended its days at Kingmoor.

The last of the class in service when it was withdrawn in December 1965, it was purchased by Richard Bill and moved to the Keighley & Worth Valley Railway on August 11, 1966. Considered too big to be of use there, it was never steamed but moved on to the newly established Dinting Railway

Centre on May 28, 1969, where overhaul commenced. It was returned to steam in 1978 authentic in LMS black livery, complete with smoke deflectors.

The main line beckoned and *Scots Guardsman* had a test run to Sheffield and back in September followed by a couple of runs to York. But apart from an appearance in steam at Liverpool Road station in Manchester in 1980 and occasional steamings at Dinting, that was it.

BR's inspection criteria on superheater flue tubes had been tightened up as a result of an incident at Didcot and No. 6115 could no longer be certified without further major work. It was eventually moved to Tyseley on September 5, 1989 but this did not prove to be the answer to the engine's problems. The death of its owner saw it being offered for sale

by his son and daughter and it was purchased initially by a trust involving Ian Storey and Mel Chamberlin for £1. However, a rift quickly emerged between various trustees and no progress was made; the Waterman Railway Heritage Trust stepped in and bought it in April 2002.

The engine was moved to Crewe but still no work was done in view of its poor condition, and in 2006, it was sold again, to David Smith's West Coast Railways, which had wanted it in the first place; moving to Carnforth on February 10, 2006.

This time, serious work started and on June 20, 2008, *Scots Guardsman* made a light engine test run, followed on July 11 by a loaded one. Now in BR green livery, it hauled its first main line passenger train for 30 years on August 16, 2008, over the Settle & Carlisle line.

RIGHT: The derelict No. 6115 at Tyseley in March 1999. ROBIN JONES

LEFT: In LMS black livery but unfinished, LMS Royal Scot 4-6-0 No. 6115 *Scots Guardsman* departs from Sheffield Midland with an empty stock test run from Guide Bridge on September 21, 1978.

ABOVE: No. 6115 *Scots Guardsman* passes Chinley on November 14, 1978. JOHN WHITELEY

ABOVE: LMS Royal Scot 4-6-0 No. 46115 *Scots Guardsman* passes Loughborough Midland with a private charter from King's Lynn on March 21, 2009.

Stanier Pacifics

Princess Royal 4-6-2

STANIER SOON realised he could improve on Fowler's Royal Scot 4-6-0s for WCML services and that a Pacific, a wheel arrangement already synonymous with the rival LNER's ECML services, was the answer. The prototype batch of three locomotives, built in 1933, are often considered to be an elongated version of a GWR King 4-6-0, with four cylinders and a taper boiler. They were very long engines, initially running with ridiculously short Fowler tenders. Even the replacement Stanier tenders were still disproportionately short, but longer tenders would have meant many turntables having to be replaced.

The first engines were No. 6200 *The Princess Royal* and No. 6201 *Princess Elizabeth*. The third prototype was constructed with the aid of the Swedish Ljungstrom turbine company and known as the Turbomotive, numbered 6202, but not named. It was one of a number of experimental variations over the years from the standard Stephenson design of steam locomotive, and one of the few to meet with any success. It was rebuilt in 1952, numbered 46202 with conventional Princess Coronation cylinders and named *Princess Anne*, but was destroyed in the Harrow and Wealdstone crash of that year.

Eleven more standard Princess Royals were constructed after the first batch, all named after Princesses. Although Princess Elizabeth was to become HM The Queen, the first engine of a class that would haul the 'Royal Scot', was named *The Princess Royal* as Mary, Princess Royal was the Commander-in-Chief of the Royal Scots. However, the engines still became known as 'Lizzies'. The design was quickly superseded by the more powerful Princess Coronation Pacific and no more 'Lizzies' were built.

Once diesels started to work WCML services, the relatively small class of Princess Royals were early casualties and were withdrawn by 1962. Surprisingly though, despite not having been nominated for official preservation, two of the class survive in preservation.

ABOVE: LMS Princess Royal Pacific No. 6201 *Princess Elizabeth* at Holyhead on September 3, 1989.

LEFT: No. 6201 *Princess Elizabeth* heads the Royal Train past Standish Junction on July 11, 2012. PETE BERRY

No. 6201 *Princess Elizabeth*

THE SECOND PRINCESS Royal, No. 6201, was completed in November 1933 at Crewe and named after the seven-year-old elder daughter of the Duke of York. Princess Elizabeth, who 20 years later would become HM Queen Elizabeth II.

On November 16, 1936, No. 6201 set the record for the longest, hardest and fastest nonstop run ever made in Britain with a steam-hauled passenger train. This was a deliberate record-breaking attempt by the LMS as part of its desire to introduce a six-hour nonstop Euston-Glasgow service. On reaching Glasgow from Euston in five hours 53 minutes, the record was achieved and No. 6201 achieved lasting fame as did its driver, Tom Clark of Crewe, who was awarded the OBE in recognition of his achievement.

After Nationalisation, No. 46201 was initially painted in mixed-traffic black livery by BR but then Brunswick green. It worked from Edge Hill and Crewe North in the 1950s but the Princess Royals were early withdrawals as dieselisation took hold and it was put in store twice at Carlisle Kingmoor in 1961-62, but returned to service again both times before final withdrawal in October 1962.

It was purchased by Roger Bell on behalf of the Princess Elizabeth Locomotive Society for £2160 and was moved on August 12, 1963 to the Dowty Railway Preservation Society's base at Ashchurch in Gloucestershire. In June 1965, it became the first LMS Pacific to be steamed in preservation, by a very wide margin.

It did not make it on to the main line though in the brief period in the mid-1960s when a handful of preserved GWR and LNER steam engines hauled occasional railtours. It did make a couple of light engine runs to open days at Bristol, Tyseley and Barrow Hill in the late 60s/early 70s, and made it to Shildon for the Rail 150 cavalcade in August 1975.

It finally took its place at the head of a main line railtour on April 12, 1976 and at this time its operational base moved to the Bulmers Railway Centre in Hereford. This run covering the whole of the North and West route, on two separate railtours, was the first time an LMS Pacific had hauled a main line passenger train for more than 12 years.

Despite its rarity value, the locomotive was not intensively used in the 1970s and, of course, from 1980 was slightly overshadowed by the main line return of *Duchess of Hamilton*. When the Bulmers Centre closed in the 1990s, *Princess Elizabeth* moved to the East Lancashire Railway, but was withdrawn for overhaul on June 13, 1993, when it initially moved to Butterley.

Both the overhaul and the engine's operational base over the ensuing years were somewhat varied, involving Rileys and the East Lancashire Railway, Tyseley, and the Crewe Heritage Centre, but always in the care of long-term society chairman, Clive Mojonner. The return to main line service, after an overhaul costing £400,000, did not come until May 11, 2002 on the WCML over

Shap; the circumstances of main line running having changed beyond recognition while the engine was out of the public eye.

Princess Elizabeth was now entering a period of much more intensive and demanding main line use and even occasional runs on heritage lines, but suffered a major setback on another run over Shap on April 3, 2004 when a core plug was dislodged causing the left-hand inside piston smashed with resultant damage to the motion.

On June 3, 2012, *Princess Elizabeth's* whistle signalled the start of the Thames Diamond Jubilee Pageant while the locomotive was standing on Battersea railway bridge, and even more significantly, on July 11, the engine hauled the Royal Train conveying the Queen from Newport to Hereford and from Worcester to Oxford as part of the Diamond Jubilee Tour.

No. 6201 was withdrawn once more for overhaul at the end of December 2012, this time, the work being carried out exclusively at Tyseley, which is expected to be the engine's normal operating base in future. It was steamed in June 2015 and is expected to be back in main line action in the spring of 2016.

ABOVE: LMS Princess Royal Pacific No. 6201 *Princess Elizabeth* departs from Crewe with a 'North Wales Coast Express' on September 3, 1989.

ABOVE: LMS Princess Royal Pacific No. 6201 *Princess Elizabeth* departs from Shrewsbury for Crewe on August 21, 1988.

LEFT: No. 6201 *Princess Elizabeth* crosses Eskmeals viaduct on the Cumbrian Coast line on October 5, 1991.

LEFT: LMS Princess Royal Pacific No. 46203 *Princess Margaret Rose* departs from Blackburn with a 'Cumbrian Mountain Express' on June 1, 1991.

No. 46203 *Princess Margaret Rose*

NO. 6203 WAS the first of the second batch of Princess Royals, built at Crewe in July 1935 and named *Princess Margaret Rose* after the then five year-old daughter of the Duke of York, the younger sister of the future Queen Elizabeth II.

It holds the speed record for the class of 102.5mph, achieved on May 3, 1936. It was allocated to various sheds during its working life on WCML expresses, starting at Camden, but working from Edge Hill and Crewe North in the 1950s before moving to Upperby in January 1962.

Originally turned out in LMS crimson lake, the engine also ran in black livery, BR blue and finally Brunswick green. It was reallocated to Kingmoor in April 1962 for its last six months of service.

Following withdrawal in October 1962, *Princess Margaret Rose* was sold to Sir Billy Butlin and after external restoration to LMS livery at Crewe, was put on static display at Butlin's holiday camp, Pwllheli, North Wales in May 1963. After a change of policy by Butlin's, the engine left Pwllheli on Sunday 11, May 1975 and after display at Derby works, arrived at the Midland Railway Centre at Butterley on November 5, 1975.

It was purchased from Butlin's in October 1988 and in late 1994, The Princess Royal Class Locomotive Trust was formed by Brell Ewart and others; *Princess Margaret Rose* was transferred into the ownership of this charitable trust and restoration commenced.

No. 46203 returned to BR metals in BR maroon livery for a loaded test run from Derby to Sheffield on May 17, 1990 and its first railtours were on the same route

on June 2, followed by a period of regular main line operation over the next six years.

The owning trust was successful in its bid to obtain another former Butlin's LMS Pacific, No. 6233 *Duchess of Sutherland*; restoration and operation of this engine has inevitably taken priority over No. 46203, as the other working Princess Coronation, the NRM's No. 46229 *Duchess of Hamilton* retired in 1996, while the other working Princess Royal, No. 6201 *Princess Elizabeth* remained active. However, No. 46203 remains on static display in the trust's West Shed at Butterley and it is hoped that it can be returned to steam in the not too distant future.

LEFT: No. 46203 *Princess Margaret Rose* heads away from Paddington with InterCity stock on March 23, 1994.

BELOW: LMS Princess Coronation Pacific No. 46229 *Duchess of Hamilton* approaches Cross Gates, east of Leeds with BR's 'Scarborough Spa Express' on August 12, 1984.

Princess Coronation 4-6-2

THE PRINCESS Coronation Class was much more than just an enlarged version of the Princess Royal; it was to become arguably Britain's premier express steam locomotive design and a firm favourite with enthusiasts right up to the present day.

They were the most powerful express steam locomotives ever to be built for the British railway network, estimated to be able to produce 3300 horsepower and with evidence to prove it.

The first five, Nos. 6220-6224, were built at Crewe in 1937; streamlined and painted blue with silver horizontal lines to match the new LMS 'Coronation Scot' train. The chief draughtsman at Derby, Tom Coleman, in Stanier's absence, was responsible for most of the detailed design including the streamlined casing. In fact Stanier had doubts about the value of this. It was not attractive in itself, but the overall effect in the livery chosen, was certainly worthwhile in publicity terms.

Before the introduction of the 'Coronation Scot', on trials just south of Crewe, No. 6220 *Coronation* achieved a speed of 114mph, beating the LNER's A4 Pacific No. 2509

Silver Link's 112mph, but entering Crewe station at a dangerously high speed and with passengers on board.

The second five, Nos. 6225-6229, were also streamlined, but painted in traditional crimson lake, with gilt lining, however, the next batch were not streamlined. Although the Second World War delayed further construction, 38 were eventually built, 24 streamlined and 14 non-streamlined, the last two to a modified design with roller bearings, by George Ivatt; the last one, No. 46257 by BR in 1948.

Nos. 6220-6234 had single chimneys when built but from No. 6235 onwards, they were built with double chimneys; the older engines receiving double chimneys between 1939 and 1944. Nos. 6245-6248 were outshopped from Crewe in 1943, streamlined but in plain wartime black livery.

Smoke deflectors were fitted to the non-streamlined engines from 1945, but in any case, the streamlining was removed from 1946 onwards. Only three locomotives were still streamlined by Nationalisation and these were treated by 1949; the de-streamlined engines initially retained sloping smokebox tops.

Postwar LMS black livery was applied after 1947 and BR blue was carried by 27 of the class from 1949, although Crewe painted some in mixed-traffic black livery (based on LNWR black), before Brunswick green became standard for the whole class.

In 1957, BR made a remarkable decision to introduce maroon livery and this was eventually carried by 16 Princess Coronations and some Princess Royals. The style was somewhat different to that of the LMS and varied between individual engines.

The class was a great success but inevitably dieselisation, and electrification of the WCML saw them lose their Top Link workings early in the 1960s with relegation to secondary duties, and after a few withdrawals, the remaining class members were withdrawn in one fell swoop in September 1964.

We are lucky that although No. 46235 *City of Birmingham* was officially preserved, though never steamed again, two more were saved by Billy Butlin. It was a long time before either returned to the main line, but without him we may never have seen one of Britain's premier express engines at work again after 1964.

ABOVE: Then newly overhauled LMS Princess Coronation Pacific No. 46229 *Duchess of Hamilton* tops Ais Gill summit on April 23, 1990.

ABOVE LMS Princess Coronation Pacific No. 46229 *Duchess of Hamilton* passes Mossley on the climb to Standedge tunnel on March 30, 1996.

No. 46229 *Duchess of Hamilton*

NO. 6229 WAS built at Crewe in 1938 as the tenth member of its class and the last in the second batch of five red streamliners, and is noteworthy in having swapped identities with the first of the class, No. 6220 *Coronation*, to travel to North America. The locomotive returned from the States in 1942 and the identities of the locomotives were swapped back in 1943.

No. 6229's streamlining was removed in December 1947 and it was painted in postwar Ivatt LMS black livery. It became No. 46229 on April 15, 1948 and acquired BR blue livery in April 1950, but then Brunswick green in 1952. In September 1958, *Duchess of Hamilton* was one of the 16 class members to be painted maroon.

Allocated to Upperby in early BR days, No. 46229 worked out of Camden from July 1952 to September 1960, then after six months at Crewe North, moved to Edge Hill in March 1961.

It was purchased by Butlin's after withdrawal in February 1964, externally restored to LMS condition at Crewe, and was moved to the new £2-million Butlin's holiday camp at Minehead in April 1964.

Duchess of Hamilton was moved away from the holiday camp in March 1975 via the West Somerset Railway's Minehead station and towed to Swindon works where it was returned to BR maroon livery

complete with smoke deflectors; LMS condition not being authentic for an engine built as a streamliner.

After delivery to York in May 1976, the National Railway Museum accepted the locomotive from Butlin's on a 20-year loan deal, and inevitably there was talk of returning it to steam. Before long, work commenced, and on May 10, 1980, No. 46229 steamed out of York at the head of a main line passenger train, the first class member to be seen in steam for 16 years.

It immediately became everyone's favourite steam engine, not just because of its design and livery; its performances quickly became legendary. Another overhaul was required after 1986 and, after purchasing the locomotive from Butlin's in 1987, the NRM duly overhauled *Hamilton* again and returned it to the main line in 1990. The engine topped Shap summit for the first time since 1964, on October 3, 1995, at a very creditable 57mph.

However, it was again withdrawn from main line duty in 1996, though not before a farewell run from Euston to Glasgow, descending Shap at a speed, "said to be approaching three figures", continuing next day to York. Its seven-year main line certificate had expired but it was able to fulfil commitments on various heritage lines for a couple of years, though it was

not in the best of condition internally or externally.

From 1998 to 2005, No. 46229 was a static exhibit in the NRM but after a couple of false starts, in September 2005 the museum announced that the engine was going to be restreamlined, returning it to its original LMS (maroon) condition.

This work was carried out at Tyseley and on May 18, 2009, No. 6229 was towed to the NRM to go on display. While a return to steam in streamlined condition has not been ruled out, the NRM has had its fingers burned financially by its acquisition, and overhaul of LNER A3 Pacific No. 4472 *Flying Scotsman* and any further involvement in main line steam running by the museum must now be regarded as extremely questionable.

ABOVE: LMS Princess Coronation Pacific No. 46229 *Duchess of Hamilton* approaches Olive Mount cutting, Liverpool with a Liverpool & Manchester 150th anniversary special on September 14, 1980.

ABOVE: Hauled by Class 55 Deltic No. 55002 *Kings Own Yorkshire Light Infantry*, the streamlined No. 6229 *Duchess of Hamilton* arrives at the Locomotion museum at Shildon on November 21, 2012.

No. 6233 *Duchess of Sutherland*

NO. 6233 ENTERED traffic on July 18, 1938, the fourth of the first batch of five non-streamlined class members to be completed. In 1943, the engine was fitted with a double chimney and in August 1946 received smoke deflectors.

Allocated to Crewe North, it was repainted in BR blue as No. 46233 in 1950 and Brunswick green in 1952. It worked from Crewe North from September 1950 to May 1958, then after being briefly reallocated to Carlisle in 1958 and Camden in 1960, No. 46233 moved to Edge Hill in September that year.

After demotion to more mundane duties as dieselisation took hold, the engine was put into store on October 14, 1963 and withdrawn in early February 1964. Along with No. 46229, withdrawn at the same time, No. 46233 was purchased by Butlin's and externally restored to LMS condition at Crewe. *Sutherland* was put on show at Butlin's Heads of Ayr holiday camp in October 1964.

Along with No. 6100 *Royal Scot* from Skegness, No. 6233 was loaned by Butlin's to Bressingham, moving between February 24 and March 21, 1971 and was returned to steam in May 1974 but only for short-distance footplate rides. In 1989, No. 6233 was

purchased from Butlin's by Bressingham.

A move to the Midland Railway-Butterley to join No. 46203 *Princess Margaret Rose* on February 4, 1996 signalled a big change in the engine's fortunes, as restoration to main line condition was now commenced by the Princess Margaret Rose Locomotive Trust, set up by Brell Ewart.

The locomotive was restored to LMS 1946 condition in crimson lake livery with a double chimney and smoke deflectors, returning to steam on March 20, 2001 and working an evening Derby-Sheffield test run July 18, unfortunately marred by an air brake failure at Dronfield. Its first full-scale railtour was on the North Wales Coast route on October 18, promoted by the owning trust.

No. 6233 made history on July 11, 2002 by becoming the first preserved steam engine to haul the Royal Train on the main line as part of the Queen's Golden Jubilee

celebrations, again on the North Wales Coast route, with her majesty travelling on some sections between various engagements. The engine also hauled the Royal Train over the Settle & Carlisle line in March 2005, this time for HRH the Prince of Wales who, at one stage, travelled on the footplate.

On September 10, 2009, No. 6233 topped Shap summit with a 632-ton train at 35.8mph, beating the class record of 30mph set by No. 6234 *Duchess of Abercorn* with a 20-coach test train of 620 tons in 1939. This proved once and for all that *Sutherland* was every bit the equal of *Hamilton*.

No. 6233 was painted in LMS black for the last months of its main line certificate during 2010, and commendably the trust carried out a public livery ballot as a result of which, on completion of a heavy general overhaul in April 2012, *Duchess of Sutherland* appeared in BR green livery as No. 46233.

ABOVE: LMS Princess Coronation Pacific No. 6233 *Duchess of Sutherland* passes Greenholme on the northbound climb to Shap summit with the Railway Touring Company's 'Great Britain' railtour on April 9, 2007.

LEFT: Princess Coronation Pacific No. 6233 *Duchess of Sutherland* departs from Holyhead with the Royal Train on June 11, 2002.

BELOW: In postwar LMS black livery, Princess Coronation Pacific No. 6233 *Duchess of Sutherland* passes Beckfoot and approaches the Lune Gorge.

ABOVE: *LMS Princess Coronation Pacific No. 46233 Duchess of Sutherland on the southbound climb to Shap at Great Strickland on September 6, 2014.*

No. 46235 *City of Birmingham*

NO. 46235 WAS ONE of the more settled members of the class, allocated to Crewe South throughout the BR period until withdrawal in September 1964. It had been designated for preservation as part of the National Collection as uniquely, Birmingham City Council had agreed to take the engine and was committed to building a museum to house it. The class leader No. 46220 *Coronation* was not considered a candidate, as it was not in as-built condition, having originally been a streamliner.

Not being one of the class members that received BR maroon livery, No. 46235 was externally restored at Crewe to BR green and moved by road to the site of the museum in Newhall Street on May 22, 1966 where the Museum of Science was built around it, the locomotive even being able to move on electrically driven rollers.

The engine was moved to a new Thinktank museum opposite the Grand Junction Railway's Curzon Street station on December 2, 2000 and this museum opened on September 29, 2001. The engine is now very poorly displayed and there are mounting calls for it to be released by the museum at least to take part in static displays of LMS main line power, or possibly even returned to steam. The museum, is however, consistently rejecting such proposals.

ABOVE: *LMS Princess Coronation Pacific No. 46235 being moved through the streets of Birmingham on December 2, 2000.*

LEFT: *No. 46235 City of Birmingham on display in the Thinktank museum in Birmingham.*

CHAPTER 17

Charles Edward Fairburn

ABOVE: No. 42085 soon after leaving Lakeside on March 6, 2005. GEOFF LEE

CHARLES FAIRBURN was born in Bradford in 1887, and studied mathematics and engineering at Oxford, obtaining a first-class degree. He then studied for two years under Henry Fowler at the MR's Derby works.

But Fairburn's career began in 1912 at the Siemens Brothers dynamo works in Stafford, becoming an assistant engineer working on the Shildon-Newport electrification of the North Eastern Railway, including involvement in electric locomotives.

Fairburn served in the Royal Flying Corps during the First World War but in 1919 joined English Electric and developed this company's railway electrification department. After involvement in several major electrification projects, including overseas, in 1934 Fairburn joined the LMS as chief electrical engineer, but was promoted to deputy chief mechanical engineer under William Stanier. It was Fairburn who introduced diesel-electric shunters on the LMS, ultimately a very numerous and long-lived design, with examples of the later developments still in service today.

Fairburn was made acting CME of the LMS when Stanier was away on war work in 1942 and became CME in 1944, on Stanier's retirement. His background was clearly not in steam yet he is associated with a numerous and popular class that survived almost to the end of steam.

In 1945 he modified Stanier's 4MT 2-6-4T giving it a shortened wheelbase, to produce the well-known Fairburn tank. Far more significantly though, he proposed the first main line diesel locomotives for the LMS, which he unfortunately did not live to see as he died in October 1945, leaving his successor HG Ivatt to oversee the first step towards main line dieselisation.

No. 42073

NO. 42073 WAS built at Brighton, for use on the Southern Region, and spent its first three months working from Stewarts Lane, before moving on to Ashford in February, 1951. It was sent to Dover later the same year, then back to Ashford again in 1952, but increasing electrification of suburban routes led to a transfer to the North Eastern Region in November 1954, allocated to Gateshead. In 1957 it worked from Bradford and Sowerby Bridge, and in 1958 from York and Neville Hill. The following year saw it at Low Moor and Wakefield, until it settled at Copley Hill, Leeds from 1960 to 1964. In 1965 it was back at Low Moor again, but transferred to Normanton for a few months up to withdrawal in October 1967.

Purchased for preservation on the Lakeside & Haverthwaite Railway, it was towed to Carnforth on April 10, 1968, where it was restored to LNWR black livery and ran during occasional open days.

It moved to Haverthwaite on November 14, 1970 just before the branch was severed and doubleheaded with its partner No. 2085 at the railway's opening in 1973.

No. 2073 was withdrawn from service in 1978 and spent some time receiving attention at Carnforth, but was returned to steam in November 2001. It has never been seen working away from the LHR.

4MT 2-6-4T

TWO-HUNDRED AND seventy-seven Fairburn 4MT 2-6-4Ts were built between 1945 and 1951, based on the earlier Stanier 2-6-4T, which was originally derived from Henry Fowler's parallel-boilered 2-6-4T. Fairburn's design basically had a shorter wheelbase and could negotiate tighter curves. Designed for suburban passenger trains, 41 of the class were built by BR at Brighton for service on the Southern Region in 1950 and 1951, replacing much older types.

This was a stopgap before BR's Standard types were introduced, as the SR was short of modern tank engines, and was a rare example of a BR region building a design from another region.

The Fairburn tanks ran only briefly on the SR but lasted on the LMR and the ER until 1967.

No. 42085

LIKE NO. 42073, this engine was built at Brighton, and worked on the SR, first at Brighton and later in the same year at Stewarts Lane, but as early as March 1952, it was transferred to Heaton on the NER and later that same year to Darlington.

1955 saw it working from Scarborough, from Whitby and Bradford Manningham in 1956 and Whitby again in 1958. It moved to York in 1959 and Darlington from 1961 to 1965, moving to Manningham before its final move to Normanton took place in April 1967, where it ended its days of BR service in October that year.

Also bought for the LHR, it arrived at Carnforth on May 18, 1968, but was restored to a rather shocking Caledonian blue livery as No. 2085. It arrived at Haverthwaite with its partner on November 14, 1970 and again worked at the reopening and the early years of the railway.

Again it spent some time back at Carnforth in the mid-1980s and returned to LHR service but its boiler ticket ran out in May 2001, just before No. 42073 returned to service. They doubleheaded in BR black for the first time in August 2003.

In BR black livery, the Fairburn tanks are popular locomotives but for many years, their owners, Charles (42085) and Austin (42073) Maher refused to allow them to visit other railways. On Charles' death, his son inherited No. 42085 so finally in 2008, the locomotive made a working visit to the Great Central Railway where repairs including the fitting of new side tanks were carried out at the GCR as part of the deal. In 2010 the engine visited the Bluebell Railway, close to its birthplace in Brighton and on a route where it had briefly worked when new.

ABOVE: LMS Fairburn 2-6-4T No. 42085 departs from Loughborough Central on the GCR in June 2008.

ABOVE: LMS Fairburn 2-6-4T No. 42085 emerges from Haverthwaite tunnel on July 16, 1994.

CHAPTER 18

HG Ivatt

ABOVE: An Ivatt doubleheader as 2MT 2-6-2T No. 41241 and 4MT mogul No. 43106 depart from Oakworth on the Keighley & Worth Valley Railway on September 14, 2012.

HENRY GEORGE IVATT, generally known as George Ivatt, was the son of the Great Northern Railway locomotive engineer Henry Ivatt. He was born in Dublin in 1886, and educated at Uppingham School.

In 1904, he started an apprenticeship at the LNWR's Crewe works and was promoted through several jobs but during the First World War, served in France. After the war, he became assistant locomotive superintendent on the North Staffordshire Railway.

When the NSR was absorbed into the LMS, Ivatt was transferred to Derby works in 1928 and after moving through various jobs including working in Glasgow was appointed as principal assistant for locomotives to William Stanier in 1937.

Stanier retired in 1944 and was succeeded by Charles Fairburn, but after Fairburn died suddenly in October 1945, George Ivatt was appointed CME on February 1, 1946, in preference to Robert Riddles.

Circumstances had changed as a result of the war; economy and ease of maintenance were the new priorities, and Ivatt continued to build existing LMS designs as the fleet needed to be updated. He built two more Princess Coronation Pacifics and more 'Black Five' 4-6-0s, all with his modifications, and continued the rebuilding programmes for the Royal Scot and Patriot 4-6-0s.

Ivatt notably designed 2MT 2-6-0s and 2-6-2Ts, and 4MT 2-6-0s, to very functional designs, totally different to Stanier's prewar style; these were to influence BR steam design after Nationalisation.

Ivatt also saw the introduction of Britain's first main line diesels, the 1600hp Nos. 10000 and 10001, built at Derby in association with English Electric. On Nationalisation though, Riddles became BR's first CME and Ivatt remained as CME of just the London Midland Region until 1951. This move quite possibly extended the life of steam traction on BR, as Ivatt could well have pushed dieselisation forward, something Riddles was not inclined to do. Ivatt's steam designs were adopted by other regions of BR for a while until Riddles' Standard steam designs started to supersede them.

George Ivatt continued in the railway industry with Brush/Bagnall until 1957 and died on October 4, 1976.

2MT 2-6-2T

THE LMS HAD various elderly tank engines and the operating department required a new small class 2 locomotive to replace them. Ivatt's 2-6-2Ts were built between 1946 and 1952 intended for light duties; this design incorporated all the labour-saving features usually found on larger engines at that time, including self-emptying ashpans and rocking grates. A tender version, the Ivatt Class 2 2-6-0 was also produced.

The LMS classified the tanks as 2P, but BR preferred the classification 2MT. Ten were built by the LMS before Nationalisation in 1948, and were numbered 1200-1209. A further 120 were built by BR, Nos. 41210-41329. Most were built at Crewe but the last 10 at Derby. Fifty engines were fitted with push-pull equipment, and the last 30 Crewe-built engines, 41290-41319, were allocated to the Southern Region from new.

No. 41298

ABOVE: 2MT 2-6-2T No. 41298 at Longmoor Downs in the 1960s . KEN LIVERMORE

NO. 41298 WAS BUILT in 1951 at Crewe, and allocated to Bricklayer's Arms on the SR in November of that year, and was mainly used on empty stock, into and out of Victoria with occasional trips on excursion trains to Allhallows.

In 1953 a transfer to the West Country brought work on the branch lines around Barnstaple until 1963, when it moved to Weymouth for boat train and local passenger turns. A final move, back to London, took place in October 1966, this time to Nine Elms where the last few months in BR ownership were spent on empty stock workings as a Waterloo station pilot.

When steam working finished on the SR in July 1967, No. 41298 was purchased directly from BR by the Ivatt Trust, and was still serviceable. It moved to the Longmoor Military Railway in Hampshire on August 13, 1967, but when Longmoor closed the locomotive was moved to Quainton Road, arriving on December 12, 1970, where a heavy overhaul commenced.

The trust built a substantial restoration shed for this engine plus another 2-6-2T, No. 41313, and a 2-6-0, No. 46447, which it bought from Barry scrapyard, but none of the three engines ever steamed at Quainton, becoming three of the longest-running uncompleted restoration projects in the country.

The Ivatt Trust came to a long-term agreement with the Isle of Wight Steam Railway that would see both the 2-6-2Ts restored for use on the Isle of Wight, 40 years after an initial plan to introduce BR Standard 2MTs to the island.

Arriving at Havenstreet on November 28, 2008, the restoration of No. 41298 was quickly completed in the workshops of the IOWSR in August 2014. It passed its final steam test on August 20, with some limited running-in completed in Havenstreet yard. A new Westinghouse air brake system, never fitted to the class in operation, has been fitted, which is necessary for its operation on the IOWSR.

ABOVE: Nearly 50 years later No. 41298 in action on the Isle of Wight Steam Railway in 2015.

No. 41241

NO. 41241 WAS built by BR in 1949 and allocated to Bath (Green Park), and worked mainly on Somerset and Dorset routes, until transferred to Wellington in October 1959 where it worked until January 1964, then Leamington for five months and Croes Newydd, ending up at Skipton in August 1965, from where it was withdrawn in December 1966.

The engine was purchased by two pioneering members of the KWVR directly from BR shortly before the closure of Skipton shed and arrived on the Worth Valley on March 18, 1967 under its own steam; ownership passing to the railway early in the 1970s.

When the engine arrived on the KWVR it was painted maroon and, along with SR USA 0-6-0T No. 72, doubleheaded the railway's reopening train in June 29, 1968. It travelled under its own steam to Shildon for the 150th anniversary of the opening of the Stockton and Darlington Railway in August 1975. In due course No. 41241 was returned to authentic BR lined black, and as well as being one of the most consistent performers on the Worth Valley has made numerous visits to other heritage lines.

The locomotive is currently stripped for overhaul with an anticipated completion date of 2018.

RIGHT: 2MT 2-6-2T No. 41312 leaves Horsted Keynes on the Bluebell Railway with empty spoil wagons for the first train of rail-borne waste from Imberhorne tip on the East Grinstead extension in June 2005.

No. 41312

NO. 41312 WAS BUILT in May 1952 at Crewe and spent its entire working career on the SR. It was first based at Faversham, then Ashford in June 1959, before being moved to Barnstaple Junction where it worked over the Torrington branch, putting in some appearances on the Ilfracombe and Exeter line.

In March 1963 it was reallocated to Brighton but the following year it moved to Bournemouth where it worked over the Swanage and Lymington branches, hauling the last steam service on the Lymington branch in April 1967. It spent the last three months of its career at Nine Elms as a Waterloo station pilot, until it was finally withdrawn at the end of SR steam on July 3, 1967.

Sold to Woodham's scrapyard at Barry, rescue for No. 41312 came on August 16, 1974 when it was purchased by a member of the Caerphilly Railway Society and moved to the former Rhymney Railway works at Caerphilly. Ten years later it was sold to John Jones and transferred to Carmarthen in 1984 for ongoing restoration with the intention being for it to work on the Gwili Railway. However, after an approach from the Mid Hants Railway, the engine was moved there in June 1996, where restoration would proceed much faster. It returned to steam in December 1998.

It gained a main line certificate after a test run on May 17, 1999 from Clapham Junction to Alton with the 'Queen of Scots' private coaching stock, after which it was used on various SR main line routes. The engine finally did run on the Gwili Railway when it visited in March 2001, and has seen action on a variety of different heritage lines between its MHR duties. It is expected to return to steam in 2016 after a major overhaul.

No. 41313

NO. 41313 WAS one of a batch of 20 engines built at Crewe in 1952. It entered service at Brighton in May 1952 but after a month was reallocated to Exmouth Junction, displacing Drummond M7 0-4-4Ts on local passenger work in the Exeter area. In April 1953 it moved to Three Bridges, but was there for only a matter of weeks before transfer to Faversham.

In November 1959 No. 41313 was reallocated to Barnstaple, but in 1963 returned to Brighton. In May 1964 it was transferred to Eastleigh, from where it was withdrawn in June 1965.

Sold to Woodham Brothers in February 1966, No. 41313 was towed to the yard at Barry where it was to stay until purchase by the Ivatt Locomotive Trust in 1975. Moved to Quainton Road in July that year, it was initially intended that No. 41313 would act as a source of spare parts for the trust's sister engine No. 41298. It was eventually decided that the engine should be restored to working order, and the trustees decided that the Isle of Wight Steam Railway would be a suitable location for their three Ivatt locomotives' future operation.

No. 41313 was moved to Havenstreet in August 2006 where some restoration work was carried out before it was placed in store.

In October 2014 it was announced that No. 41313 would be overhauled on a commercial basis at the East Somerset Railway, Cranmore with an estimated completion date of two years.

ABOVE: No. 41313 on the ferry to the Isle of Wight on Aug 3, 2006. TWS SEARLE

2MT 2-6-0

ALTHOUGH STANIER had modernised the fleet of larger engines on the LMS, the company's smaller engines were still an assortment of mostly elderly 0-6-0s, and after the Second World War, Ivatt set about modernising this fleet. As well as the 2MT 2-6-2T, he introduced a 2-6-0 tender version at the same time in 1946, which had a greater operational range than the tank engines.

Both types quickly proved successful in service, but the LMS built only 20 2-6-0s before Nationalisation. BR continued building them at Crewe but it was decided that they would be useful elsewhere on the system and 38 engines from No. 46465 onwards were built at Darlington in 1951 and allocated to the Eastern and North Eastern regions.

The last 25 from No. 46503 to 46527 were built at Swindon and allocated to the Western Region giving a total built of 128. The standard livery was mixed-traffic lined black, but Swindon later painted some in passenger lined green. Some of the green ones found their way to the LMR later in life and still carried the livery until withdrawal, which took place between 1961 and 1967.

No. 46428

NO. 46428 WAS one of the first BR-built class members, emerging from Crewe in December 1948. It moved around a lot, mainly working from north-western sheds, particularly Springs Branch, but also North Wales and the West Midlands, moving from Tyseley to Crewe South in 1966 but quickly being withdrawn and stored at Oxley until August 1967, when it was moved to Woodham's scrapyard at Barry.

In October 1979, the Strathspey Railway bought No. 46428 with the intention of using the boiler as a replacement for that on 46464. However, it was not necessary to replace No. 46464's boiler after all, and No. 46428 was purchased by the Bury Standard 4 Group, which was restoring BR Standard 2-6-4T No. 80097 on the East Lancashire Railway, moving to Bury in August 1988.

Many new parts have been made or purchased over the years for No. 46428 but serious restoration will not start until the 2-6-4T is finished, in the meantime it has been painted in red and yellow livery as James the red engine for the line's Days Out With Thomas weekends.

ABOVE: LMS Ivatt 2MT mogul No. 46428 at Bury Bolton Street on the ELR. KEN LIVERMORE

No. 46441

LEFT: In BR maroon livery, No. 46441 leaves Rawtenstall on the East Lancashire Railway in October 1995.

BELOW: Maroon-liveried LMS Ivatt 2MT mogul No. 6441 at Carnforth on the last day of regular BR steam on August 3 1968. PAUL CHANCELLOR COLLECTION

NO. 46441 WAS built at Crewe in April 1950, and allocated to Lancaster, Green Ayre until closure of the shed in April 1966 when it moved to Carnforth. On withdrawal in April 1967 it was purchased by Dr Peter Beet. It remained at Carnforth but was externally restored to an elaborate version of LMS maroon livery which made it stand out against the run-down 'Black Fives' etc towards the end of BR steam.

No. 6441 did not move to the Lakeside & Haverthwaite Railway but stayed at what had become Steamtown Carnforth, and was regularly steamed during open days. However, the owner's disenchantment with developments at Steamtown saw him move all his locomotives and stock by road to the Crewe Railway Age, No. 6441 arriving on January 3, 1980.

It returned to Carnforth in October 1990 and made a number of main line runs in the mid-1990s in less-elaborate maroon livery and carrying its BR number.

A move to the ELR came on November 30, 1993, where the engine saw regular service and eventually reverted to authentic BR black livery for a while. It last steamed in 2002, but is on static display at the Ribble Steam Railway.

ABOVE: LMS Ivatt 2MT mogul No. 46443 departs from Bristol Temple Meads for Portishead on June 2, 1985.

No. 46443

BUILT AT CREWE in 1950, No. 46443 was allocated to Derby until November 1961 when it moved to Saltley until October 1966, being withdrawn from Newton Heath in March 1967. It moved to the SVR on April 22, 1967, becoming the railway's second main line steam engine, and was a regular SVR engine for many years, even seeing considerable main line service in the 1980s.

When the SVR purchased Jubilee 4-6-0 No. 5690 *Leander* from Bill Ford, No. 46443 was offered by the railway as part of the payment. However, the members of the SVR did not want to see the engine leave the railway. They launched an appeal and raised sufficient money to buy it back, after which it became known as 'the people's engine'.

LEFT: LMS Ivatt 2MT mogul No. 46443 departs from Arley on the Severn Valley Railway in April 2002.

No. 46447

ABOVE: LMS Ivatt 2MT mogul No. 46447 at Quainton Road.
KEN LIVERMORE

NO. 46447 WAS built in 1950 at Crewe and first allocated to Crewe North shed. After only two months it was moved to Workington to join other members of the class in displacing the ageing LNWR Webb 'Cauliflower' 0-6-0s from the Penrith area. In December 1959 No. 46447 left the Lake District for Springs Branch, Wigan, where it remained until June 1960 when it was transferred to Llandudno Junction, moving on again to Bangor in September.

A year later No. 46447 was allocated to Nuneaton and then on to Derby in May 1963. From Derby it moved back to Springs Branch in May 1964 from where it was withdrawn in December 1966 and sold to Woodhams from where it was purchased by the Ivatt Locomotive Trust and moved to Quainton Road on June 7, 1972.

Restoration commenced but the trust decided that the engine's future was to be on the Isle of Wight Steam Railway and, along with fellow Ivatts Nos. 41313 and 41298, No. 46447 was transferred to Havenstreet during October 2008. However, in 2012 it was announced that, in a deal that also saw the Isle of Wight Steam Railway acquire London, Brighton and South Coast Railway E1 0-6-0T No.110 from an East Somerset Railway-based private owner, No. 46447 was to be moved to the East Somerset Railway at Cranmore for restoration to working order. The engine left Havenstreet for its new home in Somerset on October 31, 2012 and returned to steam in the summer of 2014.

LMS Ivatt 2MT mogul No. 46443 passes Llangelynen on the Cambrian Coast line on August 10, 1987.

No. 46464

NOS. 46463 AND 46464 were the last two of the class built at Crewe in 1950 and were allocated to Dundee Tay Bridge. Both locomotives took turns on pilot duties at Arbroath, and were often seen working the Carmyllie branch, becoming referred to as The Carmyllie Pilot, dependant on which one was on duty.

No. 46464 hauled the last passenger train to Brechin on August 2, 1952, the only visit to the town by a member of the class. On withdrawal in 1967, Ian Fraser, of Arbroath bought No. 46464 as his dying wish was to see it back on its home ground.

Mr Fraser had already purchased LNER D49 4-4-0 No. 62712 *Morayshire*, having worked as a locomotive engineer with the LNER at Darlington, Doncaster and Inverurie and he presented the 2-6-0 to Dundee City Corporation. Although it had been intended to put the engine on display, it was stored for several years before being loaned to the Strathspey Railway where it arrived in 1975.

It was returned to steam and hauled the railway's first scheduled passenger train on July 22, 1978 and remained in service there for several more years until suffering firebox damage when a fire was lit with no water in the boiler. The locomotive was returned to Mr Fraser's ownership and left Aviemore on November 30, 1989 for the Caledonian Railway at Brechin. Mr Fraser died in 1992 and the engine was inherited by his non-enthusiast son.

The CR decided in 2000 that it did not have the resources to overhaul the engine and the Carmyllie Pilot Co Ltd was set up to restore and operate the engine with the agreement of its owner. In March 2002 the engine was dismantled and moved to a private site nearby where long-term restoration continues.

ABOVE: LMS Ivatt 2MT mogul No. 46464 at Boat of Garten on the Strathspey Railway. KEN LIVERMORE

ABOVE RIGHT: No. 46464 at Bridge of Dun on the Caledonian Railway. IAN LOTHIAN

RIGHT: No. 46447 in action on the East Somerset Railway in 2015. MARTIN CREESE

No. 46512

BUILT IN SWINDON in 1952, No. 46512 was allocated to Oswestry until January 1965, when it moved to Willesden, then Shrewsbury, Nuneaton and finally Crewe South in June 1966, from where it was withdrawn in November.

Rescued from Barry scrapyard by Worcestershire farmer, Strathspey Railway benefactor and SVR director WEC Watkinson, the engine moved to the SVR in June 1973, but then moved on to a private site near Hereford in 1978, finally arriving on the Strathspey Railway in 1979.

No. 46512 was overhauled and worked its first Strathspey train on October 28, 2000. It was launched into traffic on February 1, 2001, named *E V Cooper Engineer* after a founding director of the Highland Locomotive Co, a subsidiary of the Strathspey Railway Co.

No. 46521

THE YOUNGEST-SURVIVING LMS-designed steam engine, No. 46521, was built at Swindon in 1953 and allocated to Oswestry, but spent most of the 1950s working from Brecon, returning to Oswestry from 1959 to 1963. It spent almost its entire working life in Wales, but was transferred to the LMR in 1962. In August 1963, No. 46521 was involved in positioning moves and overnight steam heating of the Royal Train stock, when the Queen visited North Wales.

No. 46521 was withdrawn on October 29, 1966 from Machynlleth and arrived at Barry scrapyard in March 1967. It was subsequently purchased by Charles Newton and moved to the SVR in March 1971.

After restoration, the locomotive was steamed and entered service on the SVR in July 1974 in lined-out Brunswick green livery and was in regular use until being withdrawn in August 1984. The engine was overhauled again and ran on the SVR from 1991 until December 2000, by which time it had run a total mileage in preservation of 84,031 miles, some of which was in main line operation during 1992 when it was seen on the WR and SR. After negotiations, the locomotive was moved to the GCR for overhaul by the Loughborough Standard Locomotives Group in November 2001 and is now in the joint ownership of LSLG and Charles Newton.

It was a big job, and work on the boiler alone cost more than £170,000, but the work was completed and the locomotive moved under its own power for the first time in almost 11 years just before Christmas 2011. No. 46521 is now a useful member of the GCR locomotive fleet, now carrying unlined BR black livery.

ABOVE: Green-liveried LMS Ivatt 2MT mogul No. 46521 at Highley on the SVR on September 6, 1980.

LEFT: No. 46521 at Swanwick Junction on the Midland Railway-Butterley in May 2014. MARTIN CREESE

BELOW: LMS Ivatt 4MT mogul No. 43106 works a shuttle service at Shildon, Co Durham during the Rail 150 celebrations on August 25, 1975.

4MT 2-6-0 No. 43106

AS WELL as his 2MTs, Ivatt designed a 4MT 2-6-0 for medium freight work but which was also widely used on secondary passenger services. One hundred and sixty two were built between 1947 and 1952, but only three of these by the LMS before Nationalisation in 1948. Seventy five were built at Horwich, but 50 at Doncaster and 37 at Darlington. They were classified 4F by the LMS but changed to 4MT in BR days.

With the running-plates at a high level and a gap ahead of the cylinders, but with double chimneys, many thought it was the ugliest British locomotive ever produced. The double chimneys carried by the first 50 proved to be of little use and were removed.

The class proved successful, being seen not only right across the LMR system but on the ER and NER as well. A batch took over virtually all services on the one-time Midland & Great Northern Joint Railway system in 1952, although this proved shortlived as virtually the whole system closed in 1959.

They formed the basis of Riddles' BR Standard 4MT 2-6-0, but the Ivatt ones were to last almost to the end of BR steam, gaining in popularity with enthusiasts as a result.

Built in 1951, No 43106, one of the M&GN engines, was quickly transferred away to Woodford Halse on the Great Central in July 1956. It worked briefly from Saltley in 1962, then Wellingborough and Kettering but by August 1966 was at Kingmoor. From September 1967 it was based at Lostock Hall where it became the final member of the class in service.

Its last turn was just before Easter in 1968, but this was marred by a derailment in Colne goods yard. By then, No. 43106 had been earmarked for preservation and it was fortunate that damage was minimal and easily repaired. After purchase, it managed to derail again when being prepared for a test run, but on August 1, 1968, two days before the end of BR steam, it departed from Lostock Hall for the last time, under its own steam at about 3.30pm to run via Frodsham, Chester and Shrewsbury, then Wolverhampton and Bescot to Stourbridge Junction, arriving on the SVR next morning.

The only surviving member of what became a popular class, No. 43106 has been a useful member of the SVR's operating fleet and saw main line service in the 1980s, including participation in the Rocket 150 cavalcade at Rainhill in May 1980.

A major overhaul of the locomotive was completed at Bridgnorth in 2009 and it is currently operational on the SVR as well as having visited several other heritage lines including the North Norfolk Railway where it was able to run on M&GN metals for the first time since 1954.

LEFT: No. 43106 approaches Foley Park tunnel on the SVR on December 6, 1986.

BELOW: Back on the Midland & Great Northern Joint line for the first time since 1956, No. 43106 departs from Sheringham on the North Norfolk Railway in September 2011.

BELOW: LMS Ivatt 4MT mogul No. 43106 heads a goods train away from Keighley on the KWVR on October 14, 2012.

CHAPTER 19

The future

THE STOCK of preserved LMS locomotives is not static; some have been scrapped and others could still disappear but gaps are being filled by new-build projects, of which the Fowler Patriot 4-6-0 No. 45551 *The Unknown Warrior* is the highest-profile example.

There is a serious proposal for the construction of a LNWR George V 4-4-0, but dreams of building a new LMS Beyer-Garratt or the Turbomotive are perhaps a little far-fetched. Replica construction is not new though.

L&MR 0-2-2 *Rocket*

ABOVE: The working Great Central Railway replica of Stephenson's *Rocket* approaches Loughborough Central on the GCR.

IN 1923, BUSTER KEATON had a working replica of Stephenson's *Rocket* built for the film, Our Hospitality. It was used again two years later in another film but has disappeared, although there are at least two other replicas in the USA.

In Britain a sectioned replica was built in 1935 and displayed for many years next to the original *Rocket* in the Science Museum, but in 1979 a working reproduction was built by Locomotion Enterprises for the L&MR 150th anniversary celebrations. It has a shorter chimney than the original to the clear the bridge at Rainhill. Both of these replicas are normally to be seen at the NRM, York, although the working one frequently travels elsewhere, including overseas.

A working replica of the L&MR's *Sans Pareil* was also built in 1980 and is normally on display at Locomotion Shildon, and a working replica of the L&MR 2-2-0 No. 9 *Planet* can be seen at the Musum of Science & Industry in Manchester.

LNWR Bloomer 2-2-2

PERHAPS surprisingly little known in enthusiast circles is the existence of two similar replicas of an early LNWR design of 2-2-2. Three classes were designed by James McConnell and became known as Bloomers, 74 being built between 1851 and 1862.

The nickname is said to have been a reference to Mrs Amelia Bloomer, who shocked contemporary society by wearing trousers. By comparision the engines showed more of their wheels than was fashionable at the time. Rightly or wrongly, Bloomer became the official class name.

The engines were green, although some were briefly dark red from 1861, before black was adopted as standard. The various types of Bloomers were withdrawn between June 1876 and November 1888.

A non-working replica was built by engineering apprentices for static display outside Milton Keynes station in 1991; representing the type in 1873-76 condition, numbered 1009 and named *Wolverton*. It was taken into Wolverton works in 2006 for renovation and repainting.

In addition, construction started on a working replica in original 1862 condition at Tyseley in 1986 but after a good start, the locomotive has still to be completed; work proceeding as funds and time permit.

ABOVE: Replica Bloomer 2-2-2 No. 1009 en route from Milton Keynes to Wolverton. DAVID LANGFIELD
RIGHT: The working replica Bloomer under construction at Tyseley. ROBIN JONES

Sentinel four-wheeled vertical-boilered tank

A LITTLE-KNOWN LMS locomotive class was the Sentinel four-wheeled vertical-boilered locomotive, two of which were ordered by the LMS in 1929 to work coal trains under a bridge at Radstock, which had limited clearances. Numbered 101 and 102 they became BR Nos. 47190 and 47191 but were withdrawn in 1959-60.

A group of members of the Somerset & Dorset Railway Heritage Trust at Midsomer Norton station have converted ex-Croydon gasworks Sentinel No. 7109 of 1927 *Joyce* into an SDJR lookalike, simply by lowering and modifying the cab, and it is expected to steam shortly.

ABOVE: The Somerset and Dorset Sentinel 4wVBT at Midsomer Norton.